FIRST HOME
Buying Guide

How to do it right the first time!

H. L. KIBBEY

Panoply Press, Incorporated
Lake Oswego, Oregon

Other titles in the Panoply Press Real Estate Series:

How To Buy Your First Home (audio cassette)
How To Finance A Home: Part 1 (audio cassette)
How To Finance A Home: Part 2 (audio cassette)
Selling Your Home (audio cassette)

How To Finance A Home In Oregon (softcover)

Publisher's catalog is available upon request.

Cover design: Byron Kibbey

Copyright © 1988 by H.L. Kibbey

ISBN # 0-9615067-5-X

Printed in the United States of America

Published by:
Panoply Press, Inc.
P.O. Box 1885
Lake Oswego, Oregon 97035

ACKNOWLEDGMENTS

I do my best work with a little help from my friends. To those associates who've given sound professional advice and encouraging words, my sincere thanks: Byron Kibbey, Tristania Kibbey, Tohren Kibbey, Cheryl Long, Darlene Hess, Kelly Hepner, Keith Pfohl, Ted Urton, Pat Timberlake, Katharine McCanna, KiKi Canniff, Carlie Claiborne and Janet Higginson. And a word of appreciation to those first-time buyers who've asked the questions that prompted me to write this book of answers.

Buying a home is an important transaction that should be researched thoroughly. Learn to rely on a team of professional advisors: your real estate agent, loan officer, accountant and attorney to give you the help you need. I am a real estate agent and can write only from that viewpoint. The information in this book, while carefully compiled, is not intended to be used as a substitute for competent professional or legal advice. Remember, too, that financing facts and figures are subject to change.

To my parents...

who bought one home — very successfully —
and loved it for the rest of their lives.

TABLE OF CONTENTS

INTRODUCTION

"Nothing should ever be done for the first time."

　　　　　Francis Macdonald Cornford

But then, Francis Cornford never read this book!

First-time home buyers are easy to spot. They're the ones with enough enthusiasm to set the world on fire. But they're also the ones who are filled with doubts, wracked with uncertainties, or who are just plain scared stiff. And why shouldn't they be? This is a whole new game! They've never tried it before.

Buying your first home can seem like a frightening prospect. So much is at stake — your savings, your credit rating, your financial freedom. It's difficult to get up the courage to sign on the dotted line, even if you want that home very, *very* badly.

Take heart! Fears and uncertainties are natural. After all, a home is the largest investment most Americans ever make. But like many things in life, home buying *does* get easier with practice. If you're a first-time buyer, does that mean you have to suffer through this experience, just to get the practice you need to do it right next time? Not at all! This book is designed to help you avoid mistakes the first time you buy a home. It will tell you where to begin and how to go about planning your search for a perfect home. It will take you through a step-by-step process that starts with the first gleam in your eye and leads you to your final goal — a home of your own.

Along the way, this book will answer all of the questions you're likely to ask, questions that often trouble first-time buyers. It will give you the techniques, the terminology and the timetable for success. In short, you'll learn how to save thousands of dollars and hundreds of hours of valuable time on this major investment, your home.

BUT SHOULD YOU BUY A HOME?

First things first: should you buy a home now? Or should you rent? These are basic questions that often get answered in purely emotional terms. After all, it's human nature to want a space of our very own. Wouldn't it be great to have a house to work on, with plenty of freedom to keep large dogs, hammer nails into the walls, or even paint the woodwork fire-engine red? Your emotional response is easy to gauge. Usually it's very clear-cut: either you *want* to buy a home, or you don't. If you've decided that you'd like to be a homeowner, then proceed. Take away the emotion and then answer the question on a logical basis: should you buy a home now?

If the logical aspect, the *business* of home-buying, is considered at all (and many buyers would prefer to ignore it altogether), it's often given a quick glance. One very tough, unshakable belief in this country is that real estate is a sound investment. I think it must be carved on the very cornerstone of our democracy; it's that close to being a sacred principle. So in that case, it must be equally true that home ownership is a blue-chip venture and a worthy goal for everyone.

That's where many buyers make their first mistake. Real estate is *not* always a sound investment. While there are excellent tax advantages that go along with home ownership, it does not always make good economic sense to buy a home. That doesn't mean you should cancel your hopes and dreams, and sign a twenty-year lease. Your emotional needs should not be overlooked in favor of an all-business approach. But if you understand exactly where you stand, from a monetary point of view, you will be able to plan effectively for your purchase. Your ability to 'buy smart' depends to a great extent on how thoroughly you have looked at the financial aspects of home-buying, from the actual cost of the purchase to what I call the 'aftershock'. Buyers who make decisions based only on emotional preferences often realize too late that they have made an expensive mistake.

How *do* you determine whether or not the purchase of a home makes sense? What's the easiest way to examine the whole picture, from emotions to economics? I suggest that you read this entire book *before* you go house-hunting. You'll learn how to separate whims from true needs. You'll discover how to prepare a game plan for your real estate venture, how to research effectively, choose wisely, finance appropriately and survive the whole procedure with your smile intact.

TEN STEPS TO SUCCESS

This book outlines ten essential steps in the homebuying process. In the following chapters, you'll learn how to achieve your goal by working through each step in order. Here's what you'll find:

STEP ONE:　Establish your needs and wants.

STEP TWO:　Find a good real estate agent.

STEP THREE: Determine how much you can afford.

STEP FOUR:　Establish your Target Area.

STEP FIVE:　Research new loans.

STEP SIX:　Discover other ways to finance.

STEP SEVEN: Make an offer to buy.

STEP EIGHT: Prepare for the loan application.

STEP NINE:　Understand the closing.

STEP TEN:　Enjoy your first taste of home ownership.

KEEP TRACK OF YOUR PROGRESS

The research you'll be doing is extensive and intensive—but fun! Make the best use of your research notes by organizing them in a three-ring notebook. Throughout this book, you'll find worksheets to help you record the information you gather. Use a copier to duplicate the worksheets, then add them to your notebook. You'll be collecting data from other sources, too: from your real estate agent, and loan officer, for example. Fill your notebook with all the pertinent facts and figures, then carry it with you whenever you go house-hunting. You'll find it to be an invaluable reference guide to the real estate market in your community.

By the time you've done your homework and completed all ten steps suggested in this book, you'll be astounding friends with your expertise in matters financial, geographical and even psychological. You'll have a thorough knowledge of the real estate market and loan market in your area, and you'll have plenty of confidence to back up your decision to buy that special home. Add a bit of good luck, and you're on your way!

STEP ONE

ESTABLISH YOUR NEEDS AND WANTS

"I want a house that has got over all its troubles; I don't want to spend the rest of my life bringing up a young and inexperienced house."

J. K. Jerome

Begin your search for a perfect home by making a careful assessment of the kind of a home you need and want. I recommend that you take time to do this in writing. It's an essential step, for two reasons. First, if your own goals are not clearly defined in your mind and on paper, you'll chase around in endless circles looking for a home that *seems* right. Second, if *you* aren't able to determine your requirements in a home, surely no one else can either.

In my years in real estate, I've seen plenty of would-be buyers wander aimlessly, doubling back on their tracks and hovering indecisively over the listings of homes for sale. They lose valuable time — and miss some exceptional 'deals' — simply because they don't know what to look for in a home. Wasted time and effort, in turn, add to stress, or even *dis*tress, and there's enough of that in any homebuying situation without adding extra pressure. So take time, right now, to be as specific as you can about your particular requirements.

Start with the worksheet that you'll find in this chapter: **DETERMINING YOUR NEEDS AND WANTS.** It will give you an opportunity to organize your thoughts, so that you (and later your real estate agent) will begin to form a clear description of the home that's right for you.

NEEDS: THE ESSENTIALS

The first half of the worksheet is for your 'NEEDS'. In this section, list those features you *absolutely must have* in a home, the rock-bottom essentials. Everyone has different requirements; what you find a necessity, another buyer will consider a 'take-it-or-leave-it' item. For instance, it may be vital for some buyers to be close to their workplace. My father, a busy doctor, always had to live near to the hospital, to be on hand to deliver a baby. For him, location was an essential factor in his choice, a NEED. But for most of us, a five-minute drive to work versus a twenty-minute drive is a matter of personal preference rather than absolute necessity.

Other features that buyers sometimes consider NEEDS include 'three bedrooms', 'two baths', 'a large yard' or 'space for a home office'. Some buyers must be within easy walking distance of stores, a school or transportation. Certain physical handicaps would make a one-story home a necessity. A word of caution: don't make your NEEDS list too long, and therefore too restrictive. Keep it short. Include only those items you absolutely must have in a home. Save everything else for the second half of the sheet.

WANTS: YOUR WISH LIST

The "WANTS" column is your wish list for all the special extras you'd like to have in your new home. Make this list as long and comprehensive as you'd like. Don't worry about the cost of these features right now; this is strictly window shopping! If it appeals to you, add it. Who knows what's out there waiting for you? Throw in the tennis court, swimming pool, wine cellar, or even the more prosaic non-essentials like a guest bedroom, a two-story home, or a stone exterior. By putting your

DETERMINING YOUR NEEDS AND WANTS

Needs: **Wants:**

1. _____   1. _____

2. _____   2. _____

3. _____   3. _____

4. _____   4. _____

5. _____   5. _____

6. _____   6. _____

7. _____   7. _____

8. _____   8. _____

9. _____   9. _____

10. _____   10. _____

11. _____   11. _____

12. _____   12. _____

Have you considered:

- ☐ Size (square footage) of home
- ☐ Number of rooms
- ☐ Number of bedrooms
- ☐ Number of baths
- ☐ Size of rooms
- ☐ Location of bedrooms
- ☐ Formal dining room
- ☐ Size of kitchen
- ☐ Family room
- ☐ Home office or library
- ☐ Mud room
- ☐ Basement

- ☐ Storage areas
- ☐ Garage; if so, size
- ☐ Size of lot/yard
- ☐ Trees
- ☐ Type of neighborhood
- ☐ Streets, sidewalks
- ☐ Distance to work
- ☐ Distance to shopping
- ☐ Distance to schools
- ☐ Distance to transportation
- ☐ Distance to recreation
- ☐ Space for boat or R.V.
- ☐ Handicap access

preferences on paper, you'll be much more aware of the possibilities, and so will your real estate agent.

I know a real estate agent in Portland, Oregon who spent two weeks showing homes to a couple who were being transferred there. Nothing appealed to them. They had almost decided to forget the new job and head back to Miami. Finally they came to the last few possibilities. The agent apologized as they drove to look at one home. It was attractive enough, she said, but unfortunately it had a major drawback for a family with two small children — an in-ground pool. "But we *love* a pool," chorused the buyers. "We never thought we could find one in Oregon, so we didn't think to ask." The result? A waste of two weeks and an overdose of stress. So take the time to be specific about what you'd like in your new home. Who knows what you'll find when you start to look?

If you have a partner in this home-buying venture, make individual NEEDS and WANTS lists, then compare. Try to work out any major differences on paper, so that your NEEDS lists, at least, are compatible. Those are the inflexible reqirements. Minor discrepancies from the WANTS list usually sort themselves out during the actual house-hunt.

When you've finished your list and feel that it represents your own particular NEEDS and WANTS reasonably well, make an extra copy and keep it handy. Your real estate agent will appreciate the clear definition of your requirements. And as you work your way through the next steps in the home-buying process, you'll want to refer to it yourself from time to time, to make sure you're still headed straight toward your goal.

STEP TWO

FIND A GOOD REAL ESTATE AGENT

"If you have built castles in the air, your work need not be lost; that is where they should be. Now put the foundations under them."
Henry David Thoreau

You may be tempted to skip this chapter altogether, especially if you're an independent sort with a strong do-it-yourself streak. That description fits me perfectly, and I learned the hard way that there are some things in life, notably real estate and dentistry, that seem to benefit from expert help. I strongly recommend that all first-time buyers spend time finding a competent real estate agent to guide them through their home-buying venture.

As you read this book, you'll come across many ways in which a real estate agent can save you time, or money, or both. Take financing, for instance; agents always seem to know which lender is offering the best rates and service. And when it comes to researching a neighborhood, your agent has ready access to detailed market data you'd spend days trying to unearth. Although this book will give you plenty of guidance, there is no substitute for competent professional advice.

But finding the perfect agent is sometimes easier said than done. It's not that there are so few qualified agents. In most places, you'll find plenty to choose from. The problem is finding a competent agent who will work well for you and with you. It's a question of *compatibility* as well as *capability*. An agent who works exceptionally well with one buyer may get poor reviews from another. Personalities play an important role here, as in any other partnership. And since buying a home is a major project, this could very well turn out to be a long-term relationship. So choose carefully.

HOW AGENTS WORK WITH BUYERS

Before you start your search for the perfect agent, it helps to know how real estate agents work with buyers and how they are paid for their services. Real estate firms are headed by a broker, who hires salespersons to act as agents for that company. Most states now have strict regulations that govern the real estate industry. Agents must pass examinations to qualify for a sales license, a positive change from the days when licenses were available for the asking. Now most states require a thorough knowledge of real estate law, financing and general practices before a license is issued. Brokers must pass additional exams after chalking up experience as agents.

NOT ALL REAL ESTATE AGENTS ARE REALTORS

Not every real estate firm belongs to the National Association of Realtors. Only those agents who are members of the National and State Associations of Realtors, plus the local Board of Realtors are permitted to call themselves *Realtors*. Others are simply known as *real estate agents* or *licensees*. All Realtors must agree to conform to a strict code of ethics in their real estate transactions.

WHO DO AGENTS REALLY WORK FOR?

Rumors that real estate agents work for the seller are absolutely true. It is the seller who signs a contract (known as a **listing agreement**) with an agent to market the prop-

16

erty. And it is the seller who pays the agent a commission when the property is sold. Therefore, in purely legal terms, the agent who sells a home actually works for the seller rather than the buyer. (There are occasional exceptions to this rule, as in the case where a buyer contracts with an agent to find a property, but this is not a widely used practice in residential real estate.) So where does that leave you, the buyer? All on your own, with no one to stick up for your rights? Not at all. Agents are required to be absolutely honest and candid with both buyers and sellers, a requirement most state real estate regulatory agencies strictly enforce.

HOW AGENTS ARE PAID

Most agents work on a commission basis. That is, they do not receive a weekly pay check, but instead are paid a percentage of the sales price of the home when it is sold. The commission is divided into two portions: one known as the **Listing Commission,** the other as the **Selling Commission**. Often two real estate firms are involved in a transaction. An agent from Company ABC may have listed the property (signed the agreement with the seller to market it), while an agent from another firm, XYZ Realty, may have shown the property to buyers and written their offer. In this case, Company ABC would receive the Listing Commission, while XYZ Realty receives the Selling Commission. The two agents involved are each paid a certain percentage of their company's portion.

You, as a buyer, don't have to enter into an contract with an agent when you start to look at property. There's nothing to sign. You are under no obligation to continue working with an agent who you don't feel is doing the job. You're free to switch agents each week if you like. But I know with absolute certainty that you will get the best service from an agent who is convinced of your loyalty. Finding a home for a prospective buyer takes time and energy, and the most experienced agents will not waste either on buyers who may not be around next week. Time is valuable to agents who get paid only for an actual sale.

THE SEARCH FOR A PERFECT AGENT

The loyalty question makes it very important that you choose your agent wisely. Take plenty of time to make your decision, and do your research methodically. Start by asking friends, neighbors or co-workers for recommendations. Word-of-mouth is usually the most reliable resource. Use the **CHOOSING A REAL ESTATE AGENT** worksheet in this chapter to record the agents' names, with information about their company and credentials, plus your own observations as you meet and talk with them later. You'll need to make separate copies of the worksheet to accommodate information about each agent you'll be considering.

Besides personal recommendations, there are other ways to add names to your list of prospective agents. If you're new to the area, you can develop your list from newspaper ads and For Sale signs. Choose names of agents who are marketing the type of home you think you'd like to buy, in an area where you'd like to live. Chances are, they're familiar with other homes of that style or are specializing in that particular neighborhood.

Another technique — and a good one — is to visit Open Houses on weekends. If you meet agents who seem to be a possibility, add their names to your list. When you have collected several names, it's time to interview the candidates.

Make an appointment to meet each agent individually, at his or her office. Be sure to take along your list of Needs and Wants. Explain that you are simply interviewing at this stage. Don't waste your time or the agent's by asking to look at homes now; your main goal is to narrow down your list of prospects. There's plenty you can accomplish by simply asking questions.

Start by explaining very briefly your goal and the time schedule for your purchase. Pull out your list of Needs and Wants to give the agent some idea of what you're aiming for. In your conversation, it's important to learn as much as you can about how the agent works with prospective buyers, as well as how qualified he or she is is. Try to find answers to these fundamental questions:

- Is the agent knowledgeable about this type of property, in this particular part of town? (Some agents specialize in only one area or one price range.)

- Does the agent have time to work with you? (This is especially important if you're on a tight deadline.)

- How does the agent work with buyers? What procedure will the agent follow in working with you?

Let the agent talk--- you'll learn a great deal about his or her style and your compatibilty in just a few minutes.

IS THE SIZE OF THE FIRM IMPORTANT?

The size of your agent's firm usually doesn't make a difference, as long as the company and its agent are able to offer you the services you need. One important consideration is easy access to homes in a wide area and to information about these properties.

A **Multiple Listing Service,** if there is one in your town, is one assurance of both access and information. Real estate firms that belong to such a service receive data on all homes listed by other member firms, and their agents are able to show any of these properties. That can give a two-person real estate office as much clout as a two-hundred agent firm. Not all real estate companies are members, however, and many areas of the country are not covered by Multiple Listing. Be sure to ask agents about their ability to show properties not directly listed by their firm.

CHOOSING A REAL ESTATE AGENT

Agent's name _____
Agent's firm _____
Address _____
_____
Telephone _____
Recommended by _____

The Real Estate Firm

Member of National Association of Realtors? ____
Member of a Multiple Listing Service? ____
Number of agents: ____ full-time, ____ part-time
Years in business ____
Specializes in what neighborhood? _____
Specializes in what type or price of home? _____
_____

The Agent

Member of National Association of Realtors? ☐ yes;
☐ no
Years in business? ____
Specializes in what neighborhood? _____
Specializes in what type or price of home? _____

How the Agent Works

Will the agent help me with research? _____
Will the agent help me find financing? _____
Will the agent handle all negotiations? _____
How much time will the agent spend? _____

References From The Agent

1. Name _____
   Phone _____

2. Name _____
   Phone _____

3. Name _____
   Phone _____

4. Name _____
   Phone _____

Comments / Evaluation

_____
_____
_____
_____
_____
_____
_____
_____
_____
_____
_____
_____
_____
_____
_____
_____
_____
_____
_____
_____
_____

CHOOSING YOUR AGENT

Your initial meetings will help you narrow down your list of agents. Record your observations on your worksheets and cross off names of agents who, for one reason or another, you've decided not to work with. Look again at those names recommended by friends, and add your own "sixth sense" or "gut feelings" gathered during your conversations. Choose an agent you feel comfortable with, one who is interested and knowledgeable and can offer you the service you need.

It may be helpful to you to read this book from cover to cover, before you make your final decision. You'll find mention of so many specific ways in which your real estate agent can — and should — assist you throughout the entire homebuying process. If you know what to expect from an agent, your decision may be easier.

Once you have made that decision, and are sure of your choice assure your agent that you'll be loyal. Mention that in return, you expect a continuation of the interest and guidance that made you select that agent in the first place. Live up to your part of the bargain by not looking at houses with another agent. If you see a *For Sale* sign on a home that appeals to you, ask your agent to get information on it for you. And if you'd like to look at an Open Houses on your own, tell the agent there that you are working with another agent. Your loyalty will certainly be appreciated.

But before you even set foot in a home for sale, there's still another step to take: determining how much of a home you can afford.

STEP THREE

DETERMINE HOW MUCH YOU CAN AFFORD

Median housing costs more than doubled from 1977 to 1987, rising from $44,000 to $95,000, according to a survey by the U.S. League of Savings Institutions. But a typical buyer's income more than doubled, increasing from $22,700 to $45,000 in that same period.

You've established your list of Needs and Wants, and you've chosen an agent to help you in your search for a new home. Now it's time to face those hard, cold, economic facts: just how much home can you afford?

It's wise to do this before you go house-hunting for one very important reason. What many buyers think they can afford and what the local lending institution would consider their maximum limit are often two vastly different amounts. It's discouraging to have to set your sights lower after you've found the perfect home. No modest 'starter home' will look good to you after you've tried and failed to finance the town mansion. Reality sets in with a very uncomfortable thud. That doesn't mean you can't dream a little, or aim high, as long as you know exactly where you stand and what your financing chances are.

One of the first things your real estate agent will want to do is to **qualify** you, in other words, determine what size loan you are qualified to receive from a lender. Today's home loans are remarkably similar throughout the

23

United States and certain standards apply no matter where you plan to buy. Even if you do not intend to get a new loan from a bank, savings & loan, or mortgage company, but want to try an alternate financing method (we'll cover these in Step Six), the same rules and limits may haunt you there. So ask your agent to qualify you and see where you stand.

Most agents use a very quick method of determining financial capability. After you've finished reading this book, you'll have the skills and information needed to do it yourself. You'll find a handy **LOAN QUALIFICATION WORKSHEET** in Appendix II near the back of the book. This is not an absolutely accurate approach; for the definitive answer, you'll have to visit a lending institution. But for the purpose of house-hunting, it will give you a good ballpark estimate of what you can afford.

Qualification is done by means of two calculations, both of which compare your monthly income and debts. You must satisfy each of these requirements in order to receive a loan.

RULE OF THUMB FOR LOAN QUALIFICATION

Many lenders use the following percentages to determine loan eligibility:

- monthly housing costs (principal, interest, mortgage insurance, property taxes, association dues, plus homeowner's insurance) may not exceed 28% of the borrower's gross monthly income, and

- total monthly debts (all of the above plus car payments, other loan payments, credit card expenses, alimony, child support, etc.) may not exceed 36% of the borrower's gross monthly income.

If you have a small amount of cash to use as a down payment (less than 10% of the sales price of the home),

24

you'll face more stringent lending requirements. In that case, substitute 25% for the 28%, and 33% for the 36% in the rule shown above.

INFORMATION NEEDED FOR QUALIFYING

Your real estate agent will need certain figures to qualify you. He or she is not being unduly nosy in asking for your income and debt picture; this is essential in saving time and avoiding frustration. Here is the information you'll need:

1. Your total gross monthly income from all sources (only income that is expected to continue on a regular basis may be counted; a company bonus may be included only if it is a standard occurrence each year)

2. Your car payments

3. Other loan payments (furniture, student loans etc.)

4. Credit card payments

5. Alimony or child support payments

6. Any other regular debt that will continue beyond the next six months.

If you are buying this home with your spouse or a partner, then both incomes and debts should be totaled and used in the calculations.

After a five-minute stint with a calculator, your agent will be able to give you an approximate idea of the amount of financing you might expect to receive from a lender. Add to this the amount of your down payment (the cash you will be paying in addition to the loan). The total of the two represents the estimated price of the home you can afford to buy with a new loan.

IS THAT MY FINAL LIMIT?

Not at all! I've seen too many miracles in this business to accept such rules as being hard and fast. There are many ways to finance a home, with or without getting a new loan, and there are ways to boost your buying power beyond the standards. So if you're unhappy with the results of your qualification, accept what you've learned as a starting point and keep an open mind for other possible alternatives.

Remember, too, that homes rarely sell for their original asking price unless you're in the middle of a Sellers' Market. (That's where housing is in such demand that sellers can name, and get, top price for their property, sometimes even more than the asking price!) For example, in your community, homes may customarily sell for five or ten percent below the listing price (that's the asking price). With this in mind, you'll want to look at homes priced a little higher than your borrowing limit. Your agent can tell you what the average price difference is in your area. That will help you and your agent determine the price range of homes for you to investigate.

Now the preliminaries are over and it's time to move on to **STEP FOUR** and 'zero in' on a Target Area!

STEP FOUR

ESTABLISH YOUR TARGET AREA

The average buyer spends 4.4 months actively searching for a home before purchasing, according to a survey by Chicago Title Insurance.

With your list of Needs and Wants at hand and a price range to aim for, it's now possible for you to pinpoint those neighborhoods that meet your criteria for a home. Maybe you've had your eye on one particular community all along, or perhaps there are two or three neighborhoods that offer the type of housing you want, at the price you can afford. Consider these your **Target Areas**. These are the areas where you'll focus your search.

NOW'S THE TIME TO THINK ABOUT SELLING

As you choose your Target Areas, plan ahead. It's not too early to think about the day when you'll want to sell this home. If you've taken time to buy wisely, you'll have much less difficulty selling your home later at a top price. Keep in mind that there are four factors that influence the sale of a home: location, condition, price and terms. Two of the four are within your control right now: you have the opportunity to choose the location and the type of financing for your new home, hence the terms you will be able to offer a new buyer later.

Of these four factors, location is by far the most important, and the least correctable. As you choose a Target

Area, remember that it is always a good rule of thumb to aim for the best neighborhood your price range will allow. You may be able to afford a home twice the size in a poor location, but you run the risk that its location may never improve. At selling time, your white elephant may never find a new owner — at least until you offer a bargain-basement price.

When you are evaluating a neighborhood, consider such elements as schools, parks, streets, sidewalks, transportation, shopping, utilities and cable television, plus the overall character and condition. Your real estate agent can help you compare property tax rates in different communities or you can get this information at the county tax assessor's office. If you aren't familiar with a neighborhood, learn all you can about it before you choose it as a Target Area.

Take off your rose-colored glasses as you visit a community. Look for factors that may reduce property values in that area, now or in the future. Obvious warning flags are the presence of an airport, a dump, or heavy industry nearby. Those are easy to spot. Train tracks are sometimes overlooked (especially when sellers are so accustomed to the trains, they're ready to swear that the track is virtually abandoned!) Make a note of each detail that could present a problem, then take time to check on the facts. Not every one of these warning signals automatically says "Don't Buy"; make your evaluation after you've studied the whole picture.

As you research a Target Area, look for signs of change, too. Are there buildings standing empty, or is there vacant land waiting to be developed? Is there evidence that the neighborhood is in a state of decline? Look for homes that are not kept in repair, as well as signs of abuse, such as graffiti or vandalism.

Subscribe to the local newspaper, if there is one serving the community. That's a quick way to learn what is important to area residents. Talk to people who live there, especially those whose age and family status resembles yours. Visit the Chamber of Commerce, schools, a grocery store, the library — anyplace that will give you the *feel* of the neighborhood. Your goal is to get a complete and balanced picture of properties and people who make up the community.

The **EVALUATING A TARGET AREA** worksheet included in this chapter will help you organize your data. Photocopy it so that you'll have a separate copy for each Target Area you're considering. As you're working on your research, file your worksheets in your notebook for ready reference.

RESEARCHING HOMES IN YOUR TARGET AREA

Once you've established a Target Area (or a few different Target Areas), it's time to become a real estate expert in that neighborhood. Your first goal will be to learn the statistics on each home for sale in the area. The purpose here is to become so familiar with prices that you'll be able to evaluate very easily what you feel a home in that neighborhood is worth. Study ads in the paper for homes in your Target Area, and visit Open Houses whenever possible. Ask your real estate agent for a list of available homes and information about them. Take time to have your real estate agent show you several in your price range.

It comes in handy to keep reference information on each of these homes. The **EVALUATING A HOME** worksheet included in this chapter may be copied and added to your notebook. You'll want to record the asking price, of course, the square footage, age, number of rooms, loan information, terms and general condition. Your agent may be able to give you this information from the listing files, or may have access to a computer for a print-out of all the data you'll need.

When you have seen a number of homes, inside and out, you'll start to recognize the well-priced from the overpriced properties. That's when you'll start feeling confident that you'll know a bargain when you see one!

EVALUATING A TARGET AREA

The Neighborhood
Name or location of neighborhood _____
Price range of homes _____
Property tax rate _____
Other community taxes _____
Overall appearance _____
School district _____
Deed restrictions _____

Transportation
Commuting time to _____ ; minutes: ____
Commuting time to _____ ; minutes: ____
Local mass transit: ☐ bus, ☐ train, ☐ other _____
Distance to transit stop or station: _____
Frequency of transit service: _____
Distance to freeway or major route: _____

Available Community Services
Police or sheriff _____
Fire department _____
Cable T.V. _____
Water & sewer systems _____
Street lights _____
Post office _____
Telephone service _____
Garbage collection _____
Library _____
Church/House of worship _____
Hospital/Doctor _____
Grocery store _____
Shopping mall _____
Parks _____
Swimming pool _____
Golf course _____
Tennis Court _____
Other _____
_____

Possible Drawbacks
Are any of the following located in or close enough to the neighborhood to negatively affect property values:

Airport _____
Railway _____
Freeway _____
Commercial areas _____
Industrial areas _____
Undeveloped land _____
Landfill or dump _____
Sewage plant _____
Power lines _____
Floodplain _____
Poor air quality _____
Other _____

Neighborhood Notes
How well does this neighborhood meet my needs and wants? _____
_____
_____
_____
_____
_____
_____
_____

Notes: _____
_____
_____
_____
_____
_____
_____
_____
_____

RESEARCHING HOMES THAT HAVE SOLD

For added confirmation, it's a good idea to backtrack a bit. Do the same thorough research on homes that have *sold* in your Target Area within the last six months or a year. This will not only give you background information about real estate pricing, but it will also make it easier for you when it comes time to write up an offer. If your research includes both the original asking prices and the final selling prices of these homes, you may see a pattern emerging between the two. Note whether sales prices in your Target Area are close to, or considerably lower than the listing prices. When you do make an offer to buy a home, you'll be armed with the information that, for instance, most homes in the area sell for eight- to ten-percent less than the listing price. That will help you determine a fair market value.

There are three ways to research properties that have sold — two requiring more effort than the third. First, you can obtain sales data from Title Insurance Companies or Abstract Companies. They can provide you with information they have collected from public record, although they may charge a fee for this service.

Or second, you can search the public records yourself at the County Recording Office (for sales prices and sometimes terms) and the Tax Assessor's Office (for square footage figures). Unfortunately, this is tedious work and the end results are spotty. These sources can't tell you the condition of the home, for instance — was it in need of repair or was it perfectly groomed? And that's important information to know.

The third way is the easiest by far: ask your real estate agent to give you the information. Most have the data at their fingertips; Multiple Listing Services are a goldmine of facts and figures. Real estate computer networks in some cities store detailed records of past transactions. And besides, agents who actively 'work' an area can often quote the statistics from memory. As an added advantage, your agent may be able to discover far more information than you could uncover in the public files, facts about the condition of a home and the particular terms that were offered. Use the **EVALUATING A HOME** worksheet to record this information in your notebook.

TIPS FOR SUCCESSFUL HOUSE-HUNTING

1. Keep an organized record of all your research data.

2. As you look at homes, have your needs, wants and financial capabilities firmly in mind.

3. Make sure that your agent is aware of your time schedule and expectations. Do you like to look at one or two homes in a session? Or ten to twelve? Discuss this with your agent.

4. Tell your agent about any homes you see that interest you and that you'd like to know more about. This includes homes you've "discovered" as you've explored your Target Area, or those advertised in the newspaper.

5. If you like to spend time driving around by yourself looking at homes, ask your agent for a list of *drive-bys* — homes to consider first from the outside. Your agent can make appointments later to show you the interior of those that appeal to you.

6. Plan to leave young children at home with a sitter when you look at property. You'll concentrate better if you don't have to keep a close watch on them in an unfamiliar house.

7. Express your likes and dislikes to your agent after you look at a home. Communication is essential!

EVALUATING THE HOME

Address: _____
_____

Home is □ on market; □ sold
Current listing price: $_____
Previous listing price: $_____
First date listed: _____
If sold, date and sales price: $_____
Property taxes: $_____
Neighborhood or condo association fees: $_____
Existing financing: □ assumable; balance: $_____
    type: _____
Terms offered by seller: _____
Condition of surrounding property: _____
_____
_____

Lot size: _____
Year home built: _____
Builder warranty in effect: _____
Exterior materials condition: _____
Foundation, type, condition: _____
Insulation: _____
Roof, Gutters & Chimney - type, age & condition:
_____

Types of windows: _____

Landscaping: _____
Fences: _____
Patio, Deck, Pool, etc.: _____
Garage: □ attached, □ detached, □ automatic
    opener, number of cars: _____
Other buildings (sheds, etc.): _____
Driveway: □ shared; surface: _____, width: _____

Size of home (sq. ft.): _____
Number of levels: _____
Number of bedrooms: _____
Number of bathrooms: _____

Dimensions:

Living room: _____ × _____
  Notes: ☐ fireplace, _____
_____
_____

Dining room: _____ × _____
  Notes: ☐ fireplace, _____
_____
_____

Kitchen: _____ × _____
  Built-in appliances: _____
  Notes: ☐ fireplace, _____
_____
_____

Den/Library: _____ × _____
  Notes: ☐ fireplace; _____
_____
_____

Family room: _____ × _____
  Notes: ☐ fireplace, _____
_____
_____

Master Bedrm: _____ × _____
  Notes: ☐ attached bath, _____
_____

Bedroom #1: _____ × _____
  Notes: _____
_____

Bedroom #2: _____ × _____
  Notes: _____
_____

Bedroom #3: _____ × _____
  Notes: _____
_____

Bedroom #4: _____ × _____
  Notes: _____
_____

Bathroom #1: _____ × _____
   Notes: _____
   _____

Bathroom #2: _____ × _____
   Notes: _____
   _____

Bathroom #3: _____ × _____
   Notes: _____
   _____

Laundry room: _____ × _____
   Notes: _____
   _____

Basement: _____ × _____
   ☐ finished; ☐ unfinished
   Notes: _____
   _____

Attic: _____ × _____
   ☐ finished; ☐ unfinished
   Notes: _____
   _____

Other: _____ × _____
   Notes: _____
   _____

Appliances or furnishings included in purchase price:
_____
_____
_____
_____
_____
_____
_____

Heating system: type, age, condition, annual cost: __
_____
_____

Air conditioning: type, age, condition: _____
_____
_____

Electricity: ____ amps; 220-240 volt lines for major
   appliances? _____

Water: ☐ well, P.S.I. pressure? _____; or
      ☐ community system   _____
  monthly cost _____
Water pressure: ☐ excellent; ☐ good; ☐ poor
Sewage: ☐ septic tank, size: ____ gallons
      ☐ cesspool
      ☐ community sewage system, annual cost:
_____

Defects noted by owner: _____
_____
_____

Defects observed: _____
_____
_____

Misc. Notes: _____
_____
_____
_____

Comparable homes (address, listing/sold prices):
_____
_____
_____
_____
_____
_____
_____
_____
_____
_____
_____
_____
_____
_____

WHAT CAN YOU EXPECT FROM YOUR AGENT?

In the matter of marriages or other interpersonal relationships, psychologists place *Lack of Communication* right up at the top of the list of trouble spots. And while house-hunting may not be quite as long-term as a marriage, the same rules for success apply here too.

Personal styles differ. That's why you've spent plenty of time choosing an agent who seems compatible with your personality. Now take the time to establish an ongoing pattern of communication with your agent, so that you both know exactly what to expect from each other. But what services should an agent offer you? I've discussed a few of the basics: for example, an agent should be able to give you a reasonable estimate of your buying power. He or she should help you in your research, as you choose a Target Area, a home within that area, or financing for that home.

But there's more that you can expect. Your agent should be willing to spend time and effort in locating the perfect home for you, one that meets your needs and many of your wants. Usually that means *previewing* homes to show you — actually visiting them to see if they are suitable before taking your time in showing them to you — and finding the specific financing facts on each one. Give your agent time to do this research. Or ask if you can help speed up the process by driving by possible homes and eliminating those that don't appeal to you.

Remember that your agent has other buyers and sellers to work with. One of the most frequent complaints I hear about agents is a lack of time and interest in a buyer's needs. Sometimes the cause is a different reaction speed. If you call your agent for information on a home, you may expect an immediate response, while your agent thinks tommorrow is soon enough. Other times, the problem is simply poor communication, leading to a difference of expectations. Communicate with your agent right from the start so that you know how much time he or she can devote to you and in turn learn what your agent expects from you.

WORKING WITH FSBOs

Have you heard the term **FSBO** (pronounced *Fizz-bo*)? It comes from the first letters of the words "For Sale By Owner", and in real estate circles it refers to a person who is selling his or her home without the help of a real estate agent. FSBO can also refer to the home itself.

Buyers are often a little uncomfortable with the prospect of a FSBO in the neighborhood. They've sworn their undying loyalty to their agent, but here's a home that appears to be outside the agent's scope. Should they ignore the FSBO, hope it isn't the world's best bargain, and stick to homes listed with real estate firms? Or should they deal with the owner directly? The best course of action is to be perfectly honest with your agent. Tell your agent about the FSBO and ask if he or she would contact the owner and find out more about the home. I've found that most owners will cooperate with an agent without increasing the asking price. If not, then your agent will put the decision to look or not to look at that home in your hands. No matter what you decide to do, your relationship with your agent won't suffer from guilt or disloyalty.

HOW TO REALLY LOOK AT A HOME

When you find a home worth looking at twice, it's time to get down to the nitty gritty details of construction and condition. Don't let Love At First Sight blind you to obvious, and not-so-obvious defects. Try to look past the marketing techniques sellers use to enhance their product: soft music, flattering pink light bulbs, the tantalizing aroma of homemade bread and the absence of any human clutter. Don't be fooled into thinking that a home that looks, and smells, and sounds this good must be perfect, inside and out. Some very costly problems could be lying in wait for you. Now's the time to find them.

As you take a serious second look, spend time opening cupboard doors, turning on faucets, looking under, over and behind furnishings that could be hiding cracks or damage. The **EVALUATING A HOME** worksheet will give you a place to start. But even a careful examination may fail to uncover defects. Be sure that your real estate agent asks the seller if there have been any problems with the home in the past and what, if anything, was done to correct them. Don't be hesitant to ask for more information.

If you have doubts about the condition of a home, or if you would feel more secure with a professional opinion, consider hiring a home inspection firm to look for problem areas. Real estate agents are not, as a rule, home inspection experts. They may pass along information from the seller concerning defects, and may even voice a few concerns of their own. But their job is not to give you a qualified opinion of a home's condition. They can, however, often direct you to home inspection services operating in your Target Area. Since most buyers prefer to ask for an inspection at the time an offer is written, I'll cover the how-tos of inspections later in this book, in **STEP SEVEN: MAKE AN OFFER TO BUY**.

Right now, while you're hard at work researching your Target Area and searching for the perfect first home, take time to begin another chapter in your information notebook. It's not a bit too early to begin **STEP SIX: RESEARCH NEW LOANS**. By the time you're ready to make an offer on a home, you'll know exactly where the funds will come from.

STEP FIVE

RESEARCH NEW LOANS

The average homeowner stays in a home only five or six years. In fact, each year 17% of Americans move. Most home loans are repaid before reaching their full term.

There are dozens of ways to finance a home. Your next research assignment will be to find the one financing method that will work best for you. Not for your neighbor. Not for your brother-in-law. Not for your boss's second cousin. What works for them may be perfectly disastrous for you. The secret is to study all the financing possibilities until your choice becomes quite clear. Then go for it!

I like to divide financing methods into two distinct groups: financing with or without a new loan. In this chapter, **STEP FIVE**, you'll explore the loan market. You'll discover what type of loans are being offered today, and how to evaluate their costs as well as their benefits to you. Then in **STEP SIX** you'll find many alternate ways of financing your new home, opening up an exciting range of possibilities. After you've researched your way through both chapters, your choice won't seem at all overwhelming. Your best financing method should be quite apparent.

RULES TO CONSIDER WHEN FINANCING

1. Choose the type of financing that is best suited to your income and financial requirements. Don't be swayed by financing fads. A loan that is right for your neighbor may be a poor choice for you.

2. Research government loan programs. They offer favorable interest rates and are sometimes easier to qualify for than conventional loans.

3. Once you have decided what type of financing you want, comparison shop for the best possible interest rates, loan fees, terms and conditions.

4. Avoid the need to refinance later. Each time you take out a new loan, you will "lose" a considerable amount of money in the form of loan fees and closing costs. It may be less expensive in the long run to choose a permanent method of financing at a slightly higher interest rate than one which will force you to refinance in a few years.

5. Plan for the future. If possible, choose financing with terms that will be acceptable to you five or ten years from now. If assumability or the right to sell your home on contract is important, find a loan that includes these provisions.

FINANCING YOUR HOME WITH A NEW LOAN

Loans are available from many sources: banks, savings and loan associations, thrifts, mortgage companies, credit unions, government agencies and generous parents, to name a few. No matter which of these you choose, you'll see certain similarities. For example, any loan has two elements: first, there's the **interest rate**. That is the cost of the money you borrow and is usually expressed as a percentage of the loan amount. Think of this as the profit your lender makes from the loan.

The second element of a loan is **time** — the length of time you have to repay the loan and the interest. This is called the **term** of the loan. By varying one or both of these elements, interest rate and time, entirely new kinds of loans are produced. Later in this chapter you'll see how lenders have added variety (but also complication and confusion) to the loan market.

It wasn't always this way. Up until the late 1970s, financing a home was a relatively simple procedure. There were very few decisions for the homebuyer to make, since the loans offered by different lending institutions were quite similar. Most were long-term loans with equal monthly payments and a fixed interest rate that was low enough to avoid a serious case of buyer anxiety. Those were the 'good old days'!

All of a sudden the loan picture changed. Rapidly increasing inflation of the late 1970s brought growing dissatisfaction to the financial community. Interest rates on home mortgages, which had fluctuated very little over the previous 30 to 40 years, suddenly increased drastically. For example, the interest rate on FHA loans first reached the double digits (10%) in April 1979. By September 1981, less than 2½ years later, it had soared to 17.5%.

No wonder the lenders were uncomfortable! Those who had loaned money to borrowers at 6% interest on fixed-rate 30-year loans were locked into that meager 6% return on their investment for the remainder of the 30 years (or until the loan was repaid). Homebuyers weren't happy either; few could qualify for a loan at 17.5% interest, even if they were willing to take on such a steep debt. The result was a stalemate, and as the number of borrowers dwindled, both sides suffered. The lenders were stuck with their old, unprofitable loans, while a large percentage of Americans could not afford to buy a home.

That's when the resourceful lenders worked on compromise plans. They experimented by making changes in one or both of the two basic elements of a loan — the interest rate and term — until new loan varieties emerged. These new loans satisfied the lenders' investment needs, while making financing affordable and attractive for the homebuyer.

Fortunately our interest rates did not remain sky-high. They gradually returned to tolerable levels. But many of the new affordable financing techniques stayed with us, giving buyers a much wider choice in housing loans. That's good news for first-time buyers, who often list 'affordability' as a major requirement.

However the less-than-good news is that borrowers are faced with an often confusing array of loans. It's not un-common for a lender to offer thirty, sixty-five or even a hundred and fifty different loan variations! The choice has become difficult for borrowers who don't know what to expect when they talk to a loan officer. Advance knowledge certainly helps. The purpose of this chapter is to give you a head start in your financing research, so that you'll be able to concentrate on those types of loans that will suit your needs best.

CONVENTIONAL AND GOVERNMENT LOANS

Housing loans can be divided into two groups, depen-ding upon their source: conventional and government loans. The term **conventional loan** refers to any loan in which the government doesn't offer, insure or guarantee funds. These are loans from the private sector, from len-ding institutions such as banks, savings and loan associa-tions, thrifts, mortgage companies or credit unions. These conventional loans are known as **institutional** loans. Also included in the category of conventional financing are loans from private individuals, such as your parents or a friend.

Government loans, on the other hand, are loans whose regulation or funding is carried out by an agency of government. While Federal Government programs such as those from HUD, the Veterans Administration and the Farmers Home Administration are popular throughout the United States, many state and local governments also offer excellent programs. Later in this chapter, you'll have a closer look at government loans and their advantages or disadvantages for you.

HOW TO SPEAK THE LANGUAGE

There are some basic terms and ideas that are common to all types of loans. When the time comes for you to apply for financing, words like *amortization*, *LTV* or *LVR*, and *PMI* will roll off your loan officer's tongue. Even seasoned buyers have been known to feel intimidated by the strangeness of it all. So here's a map through the unfamiliar territory of lending language.

Amortization
Most residential real estate loans are amortized loans. The word **amortize** means to repay a loan in equal monthly installments. Therefore an amortized loan has equal monthly payments for the agreed-upon term. Included in each payment will be a portion to pay the interest that is due, and a portion to reduce the principal balance (that's the amount you borrowed). Payments are calculated exactly so that at the end of the loan term, all of the interest has been paid and the loan balance is reduced to zero. Loan officers use what is known as an **Amortization Chart** to calculate what these equal monthly payments will be.

Mortgage Loan
If you walk into a lending institution and ask for a mortgage, you won't get one. Negative thinking? Not at all. You won't get a **mortgage**, but you may, in fact, get a **mortgage loan**. Your lender will get the mortgage.

Confused? You're not alone! Many people don't know quite what a mortgage is. It isn't a loan; instead it's a document that offers security or collateral for a loan. The mortgage document gives the lender the right to obtain title to the property if you fail to live up to your part

45

of the loan agreement. In most real estate financing, the home is used as collateral for the loan. You get the mortgage loan; you give the lender a mortgage. Today most conventional lenders use another type of security document known as a **trust deed**, in place of a mortgage. But the word mortgage has remained in our vocabulary.

Down Payment

When you buy a home, most lenders expect you to invest some of your own money towards the purchase price. This contribution is your **down payment**. The sum of the down payment plus your financing equals the purchase price of your new home. How large a down payment should you have? Or how small a down payment can you squeak by with? Conventional lenders usually require at least a 5% down payment. If you have less than that, a government loan or alternative financing method may be your best solution. But do read the section on conventional loans too, for basic financing information.

Loan-To-Value Ratio

Lenders prefer big, hefty down payments — that is, down payments equal to 20% or more of the purchase price of the home. That doesn't mean they'll turn aside a prospective buyer will less cash. But they do offer certain benefits to borrowers with larger down payments. The reason for this shows up in the lending industry statistics: traditionally, buyers with a small down payment — say, 5% or so — are far more likely to abandon their investment when times get tough than owners who have contributed a larger down payment. It's quite a bit easier for borrowers in financial difficulty to walk away from a $5,000 investment than from $20,000.

So the size of your down payment is important to your loan officer. But while we talk in terms of down payment amount, loan officers see the flip side of the coin, the **Loan-To-Value Ratio**, also known as the **LTV** or **LVR**. Loan-To-Value Ratio is the amount of your loan compared to the value of the home. It's expressed as a percentage. Let's assume you're planning to buy a $100,000 home with a $20,000 down payment. To determine your LTV, first calculate the size of loan you'll need:

Value of the home:	$100,000
Down payment:	– $ 20,000
Loan needed:	$ 80,000

Now we can determine the Loan-To-Value Ratio:

$$\text{LTV} = \frac{\text{Amount of Loan}}{\text{Value of Home}} \times 100\%$$

$$= \frac{\$80,000}{\$100,000} \times 100\%$$

$$= 80\%$$

If, instead, you had a $10,000 down payment, then your LTV would be 90%. The larger the down payment, the lower your Loan-To-Value Ratio.

In order to simplify things, conventional lenders group LTVs into certain broad categories. Standard categories are 95%, 90% and 80% LTV. Here's how the loans are grouped:

Down Payment	Calculated LTV	LTV Category
5% to 9.99%	95% to 90.01%	95% LTV
10% to 19.99%	90% to 80.01%	90% LTV
20% and over	80% and lower	80% LTV

For example, even if your down payment equals 19% of the value of the home, your loan will still be considered a 90% LTV loan. In terms of special benefits, you'll be treated exactly like the borrower who has a 10% down payment. Until you pass that 20% down payment mark, you will not be given the benefits accorded 80% LTV borrowers. If you're close to a better LTV category, ask your loan officer what advantages would be gained by increasing your down payment.

Private Mortgage Insurance

Private Mortgage Insurance, or **PMI**, is as popular among borrowers as the common cold. And just as unavoidable for many! PMI is an insurance policy that protects the lender against loss suffered should the borrower default and foreclosure become necessary. It does not protect the borrower in any way. PMI is required on most, if not all, conventional loans with a loan-to-value ratio over 80% and on some loans that are riskier for the lender, over 75% LTV.

The cost of the insurance is what makes borrowers groan for they are the ones who foot the bill. the premium is based on the type of loan (fixed-rate, adjustable-rate, etc.) and the loan-to-value ratio. Loans that carry a higher risk for the investor (lender) will have more expensive premiums. In other words, 95% LTV loans will cost the borrower more to insure than 90% LTV loans, and the PMI on adjustable-rate loans will be costlier than that on fixed-rate loans.

Traditionally, payment of the first year's premium has been required at closing, when the final purchase documents are signed. Each month thereafter, $\frac{1}{12}$th of a year's premium will be added to the regular monthly loan payment. Now, however, some lenders are offering loans with mortgage insurance that is financed along with the principal itself. This eliminates the need for extra cash at closing and is an option that is worth considering.

While PMI costs and requirements vary slightly from lender to lender and from loan to loan, here are some sample costs:

Sample 30-year Loans Amount, Type, LTV	Premium Paid At Closing	Monthly Premium
$50,000 fixed-rate 80%	$125	$10
$50,000 fixed-rate 90%	$450	$12
$50,000 fixed-rate 95%	$650	$15
$50,000 adjustable 80%	$325	$16
$50,000 adjustable 90%	$450	$18
$50,000 adjustable 95%	$750	$18

48

You'll notice that the first year's premium is larger than that for the second year. In some policies, the premium may decrease slightly in the later years of the loan. Your loan officer can give you the specific costs and requirements for a loan you are considering.

Mortgage insurance is an inevitable part of the conventional loan market. The only way to avoid it is to make a down payment of 20% or more, or to choose a type of non-conventional financing that does not require it.

CHOOSING A CONVENTIONAL LOAN

You'll have an easy time sorting out loan variations if you understand the three most common types of loans on the market today:
- the fixed-rate 30-year loan
- the fixed-rate 15-year loan, and
- the adjustable-rate mortgage loan.

The dozens of loan options you'll encounter as you shop for financing will no doubt be variations on one of these three basic themes.

THE 30-YEAR FIXED-RATE LOAN

Definition: **A conventional, fixed-rate 30-year loan has an interest rate that does not vary over the life of the loan.* It has equal monthly payments that include both principal and interest and is fully amortized. This means that the monthly payments have been calculated so that all principal and interest due will have been completely paid by the end of the thirtieth year.**

*Loan documents often list specific circumstances under which the interest rate may increase. These might include sale, lease or transfer of interest in the property, or failure to meet the conditions of the loan agreement. Exceptions vary from loan to loan. Be sure to study all loan documents thoroughly.

The 30-year fixed-rate loan has long been the most popular financing for homes. I like to call it "Old Faithful" because it's been the backbone of the home loan market for many years. But there's another reason, too: Old Faithful is a steady, even-tempered loan. Both the interest rate and the monthly payments remain the same for the entire term of the loan. There are no surprises or unexpected changes here. That's why homeowners like this thoroughly predictable loan; they know exactly what they'll be paying each month five, ten or even thirty years from now.

HOW TO CALCULATE MONTHLY PAYMENTS

It's easy to determine what your monthly payments will be on a 30-year fixed rate loan (or other types of financing) by using an amortization chart. You'll find one in **APPENDIX I** near the back of this book.

First, ask your real estate agent or a loan officer what the current interest rate might be on a fixed-rate 30-year loan. As an example, we'll assume a rate of 10%. If you turn to the Amortization Chart, you'll notice that interest rates are across the top of the chart, with the term of the loan, in years, down the left side. Now find the column that corresponds to the interest rate on the loan, in our example, the column marked '10.00'. Follow down that column until you come to the 30-year point. You'll read '8.78', which, in dollars, is the monthly payment for each $1,000 borrowed at 10% for a 30-year loan: $8.78. Now simply multiply this figure by the amount of your loan, expressed in thousands. For example, if you borrow $50,000, multiply 50 by $8.78. Your monthly payment will be $439. If, instead, you decide to borrow $55,000, simply multiply 55 by $8.78, giving you a monthly payment of $482.90.

If your loan is for an uneven amount, $54,985. for instance, move the decimal point three places to the left (54.985) and multiply this figure by $8.78 to determine your monthly payment.

Monthly payments on loans may also include 'extras'. First of all, there may be Private Mortgage Insurance. Then your lender may require a reserve account for property taxes and/or homeowners' insurance. In that case, your monthly payment will include $\frac{1}{12}$th of the estimated annual property taxes and $\frac{1}{12}$th of the insurance premium. Think of a reserve account like the Christmas Club accounts some banks offer. Here's how they work: if you think you'll need $300 to spend next Christmas, you make twelve monthly $25 payments during the preceding year. By December, the $300 is waiting for you! In a home loan reserve account, your lender will estimate the amount needed for taxes and insurance, and add $\frac{1}{12}$th of this to your monthly payment. While each lender or loan has different requirements, reserve accounts are often mandatory on 95% and 90% LTV loans, and on many other loans as well.

ADVANTAGES OF A 30-YEAR FIXED-RATE LOAN

Old Faithful deserves its nickname for some very good reasons:

1. The 30-year fixed-rate loan is stable and predictable; the monthly payments never vary.

2. The interest rate remains constant over the term of the loan. No surprises here!

DISADVANTAGES OF OLD FAITHFUL

So far it sounds perfect. What's the catch? Although this is an excellent loan there are some disadvantages to consider:

1. The interest rates charged by lenders for this loan are slightly higher than for other types of loans.

2. Higher interest rates mean higher monthly payments (at least initially) than for some other loans.

3. Higher monthly payments, in turn, require a larger income to qualify. Other loans are more affordable.

4. The interest rate will remain the same for 30 years. An advantage if you're happy with it; a disadvantage if market rates drop.

USE THE 30-YEAR FIXED-RATE AS A STANDARD

Most homebuyers consider a 30-year fixed-rate loan first. If they find that they can easily qualify for the payments, they may opt for a shorter-term loan (15-year loans are popular now) to reduce the amount of interest paid. On the other hand, if they cannot qualify for a large enough 30-year fixed-rate loan, they can turn to the 'affordable' variations: adjustable-rate loans or buydowns.

THE 15-YEAR FIXED-RATE LOAN

Definition: **A conventional 15-year fixed-rate loan is similar to the 30-year fixed-rate loan, but with a shorter term. It has an interest rate and amortized monthly payments that never vary over the life of the loan.**

By changing one of the two basic elements of a loan — in this case, the term — we get a different type of loan, with the stability and predictability of the 30-year fixed-rate loan, but with some characteristics all its own. Old Faithful's popular cousin, the 15-year fixed-rate loan, may be excellent financing for those buyers who can easily qualify for a loan and who can afford to make larger monthly payments. But what sensible borrower would voluntarily opt for higher payments? And even more important, why? The answer is interest. Because this loan is amortized over a shorter term — fifteen years

52

instead of thirty — the borrower saves a considerable amount of interest. Actually more than fifteen years' worth!

Another advantage of the 15-year loan is what we call **rapid equity build-up**. **Equity** is that portion of the value of your home that you actually own, free and clear. It is the total value of your home minus your loan balance. Homeowners increase their equity in two ways: first, with an increase in the value of their home through improvements or inflation; and second, by reducing their loan balance. With a 15-year loan, the loan balance is reduced quickly and this produces a increase in equity.

To see how that happens, it's necessary to understand how a 15-year fixed-rate loan compares to its 30-year counterpart. Let's use as an example two $50,000 fixed-rate loans, both at 11% interest. One is a 30-year loan, the other a 15-year loan. Using the amortization chart in **Appendix I**, you'll find, in the 11.0% column, that the factor for the 30-year loan is 9.52, while the factor for the 15-year loan is 11.37.

From this we can calculate the monthly payments of each:

30-year loan: 9.52 × 50 = $476.00
15-year loan: 11.37 × 50 = $568.50

You can see that **the shorter the term of a loan, the higher the monthly payments**. But the payments on the 15-year loan are not as high as you might expect. They aren't double, even though you have only half the time in which to repay the loan. In fact they're usually only 15 to 20 percent higher than payments on a similar 30-year loan. You can see that the slightly higher monthly payments will result in a quicker repayment. But it's necessary to go a step further, taking a look at the total interest paid on each, to find an astounding difference.

The interest charged on a loan is determined by three things: the interest rate, the amount of money still owed (that's the principal or loan balance), and the time period for which the interest is to be calculated (usually monthly for standard residential real estate loans). In our two sample loans, the three factors start out the same for each loan: an 11% interest rate, $50,000 loan balance and interest to be calculated monthly. So here is the first month's interest charge on each loan:

Amount of interest = **rate (as a decimal) x principal**
x period (in years)
= .11 × $50,000 × 1/12
= $458.33

Therefore, on both the 15-year and the 30-year loans in our example, the first month's interest payment will be $458.33. The remainder of the payment will reduce the principal balance.

Type of Loan	Monthly Payment	Interest Due	Toward Principal	New Loan Balance
30-year fixed-rate	$476.00	$458.33	$ 17.67	$49,982.33
15-year fixed-rate	$568.50	$458.33	$110.17	$49,889.83

Already, after just the first payment, there's a considerable difference. Because the larger payments on the 15-year loan allow more to be applied toward reducing the principal, the loan balance on the 15-year loan is noticeably lower after just the first payment. And this lower principal affects the second month's interest payment on both loans. Since the loan balance on the 15-year loan is now less than that of the 30-year loan, the interest due for the second month will be slightly less on the 15-year loan. That leaves even more of the monthly payment to be applied toward the principal.

At the end of fifteen years, the principal on the 15-year loan has been reduced to zero, while the loan balance on the 30-year loan still hovers around $42,000! And even more amazing is the total amount of interest paid over the full term of each loan: approximately $52,000 interest on the 15-year loan, and a whopping $121,000 interest on the 30-year loan! That's a savings of nearly $70,000!

54

And if that weren't sufficient inducement to apply for a 15-year loan, consider this: lenders usually offer a slightly lower interest rate (one-quarter to one-half a percentage point) on their 15-year loans than that charged for 30-year loans. This results in an even greater interest savings over the term of the loan.

THE 15-YEAR LOAN ISN'T FOR EVERYONE

Since the size of loan you are qualified to obtain is based on your monthly payments versus your income, you will not qualify for as large a 15-year loan as for a 30-year loan. If qualification is a problem, you'd be wise to look for a more affordable loan.

Another possible drawback to the 15-year loan is rapid equity build-up. Just a minute! Wasn't that one of its advantages? Well, yes — to many homeowners a large equity is an asset. For others it may be financially unwise. Equity in a home is not quite like money in the bank. Unlike funds in a savings account, equity in a home cannot be withdrawn when you need it. If the real estate market is in the doldrums and interest rates are high, you may have difficulty cashing in on your equity. In a tough selling market, homes with readily assumable high LTV loans sell faster than those where a brand new loan or large down payment is required.

ADVANTAGES OF A 15-YEAR FIXED-RATE LOAN

As you can see, there are plenty of reasons for choosing a 15-year loan:

1. It's a stable, predictable loan; the monthly payments never vary.

2. The rapid equity build-up appeals to many buyers.

3. There is a considerable interest savings over the term of the loan.

4. Lenders usually offer a slightly lower interest rate on 15-year loans.

DISADVANTAGES OF A 15-YEAR LOAN

1. Monthly payments are higher than those for other loans.

2. It requires more income to qualify for a 15-year loan. Or looking at it a different way, you can qualify for a larger 30-year loan than for a 15-year loan.

3. Rapid equity build-up may make it harder to resell the home in a difficult market.

COMBINE THE BEST OF BOTH LOANS

There is a way you can take advantage of the quick payoff feature of the 15-year loan, plus the corresponding savings in interest, without having to qualify for the higher monthly payments. Simply choose a 30-year loan but make higher payments than required each month. If you increase the size of your payments to match those of a similar 15-year loan, your loan will be paid off in fifteen years and you'll save a tremendous amount of interest. Another benefit is that you are not committed to making the larger payments, as you would be if you chose the 15-year loan. You may revert to the standard smaller payments at any time.

If this approach sounds appealing, discuss it with your loan officer when you apply for a loan. Some loan documents contain a clause forbidding a borrower to make larger monthly payments. Most lenders, however, are quite happy to accommodate you in this request.

WHEN YOUR GOAL IS AFFORDABILITY

So far, you've studied the two most popular fixed-rate loans. Both types rate high marks in *stability* and *predictability*, but they fall short of perfection in one area: *affordability*. The following loans and financing techniques were designed to meet the needs of borrowers who have difficulty qualifying for a sufficiently large 15-year or 30-year fixed-rate loan. But there are other reasons, too, for their popularity. Read on!

THE ADJUSTABLE-RATE MORTGAGE LOAN

Definition: **An adjustable-rate mortgage loan has an interest rate that fluctuates according to a specified index. The rate is adjusted, and corresponding changes are made in the monthly payments, at prearranged intervals over the life of the loan.**

When adjustable-rate mortgage loans (otherwise known as **ARM loans** or **ARMs**) first gained widespread attention in the early 1980s, borrowers were skeptical. Obviously ARMs were of great benefit to the lenders, since the interest rate could be adjusted to meet the drastic increases we were seeing at that time. But were they of any help to the borrower? In an immediate way, yes. Because the lenders could be assured of periodic rate increases, they were — and are — able to offer ARM loans at considerably lower interest rates than those for fixed-rate loans. (ARMs rates are often 3% lower!) Not only was this appealing, since monthly payments, too, were correspondingly lower, but it also made ARMs much easier to qualify for. As interest rates continued to climb, a few tentative buyers took the plunge; they found that the only loan they could afford was an ARM.

The early ARM loans were a little frightening. Monthly payments could soar or dip all over the amortization charts. No wonder borrowers were hesitant!

Fast-forward to the late 1980s: within a very few years, adjustable-rate mortgage loans gained acceptance and respectability. Today's ARMs are gentle, restrained, and increasingly popular among homebuyers. Lenders still benefit, of course, but borrowers are seeing the advantages too. Some choose an ARM loan for affordability; others because it simply makes good economic sense for them.

HOW AN ARM WORKS

All adjustable-rate mortgages have four factors in common:

- **Period of Adjustment:**
  This tells how frequently the interest rate will be adjusted. For example, with a 1-year ARM, the interest rate will be adjusted each year. You'll find a variety of ARMS, with adjustment periods from 6 months to 10 years.

- **Note Rate:**
  This is the initial interest rate the lender will charge for the first period of adjustment.

- **Index:**
  This is the guideline that is used as the basis of adjustment. Different indexes are used, a common one being the 1-Year U.S. Treasury Index. If the index rate (for example, the Treasury Index) has increased at the time of adjustment, the interest rate on your ARM will be raised accordingly.

- **Margin:**
  To determine the interest rate on an ARM loan, the lender adds to the index rate a few percentage points called the **margin**. The margin will always stay the same over the life of your loan, although margins differ from loan to loan. The interest rate on your ARM loan equals the index rate plus the margin. For example, if the index is at 8% on the day you obtain your

58

loan, and your margin is 2%, then your ARM loan interest rate will be 10%. At the time of adjustment, if your index rate has increased to 9%, then your interest rate will be raised to 11% (9% plus the 2% margin).

This chart shows how the interest rate on an ARM loan is adjusted. Notice that fluctuations in the index only affect the ARM's rate at the time of adjustment.

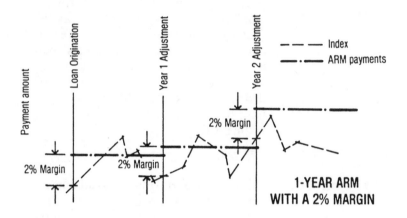

SAFETY DEVICES OFFER PROTECTION

Today's ARM loans are kept on a good sturdy leash. While their payments are not as predictable as those for 15- and 30-year fixed-rate loans, they are kept well under control by means of safety devices called **Caps**. This avoids the syndrome known as **Payment Shock**, the affliction suffered by many borrowers who were not protected from extreme payment increases. Here are some safety features to shop for in an ARM:

• **Lifetime Cap:** This is the maximum percentage of interest increase or decrease that may occur during the term of the loan. For instance, a 5% lifetime cap on an ARM

59

with a note rate of 10% means that the interest may never exceed 15% or drop to less than 5%.

- **Adjustment Cap:** This is the maximum percentage of interest increase or decrease that may occur at the time of adjustment. On 1-year ARMs it is often called the **Annual Cap**. A 2% adjustment cap on an ARM with a note rate of 10%, for example, means that the interest at the first adjustment may not be increased above 12% or decreased to less than 8%. On each succeeding adjustment, an additional 2% may be added (or deducted). Most ARM loans today have both a Lifetime Cap and an Adjustment Cap.

- **Payment Cap:** This is an option that is available on some ARMs, but is losing popularity, in favor of the Lifetime and Adjustment Caps. A Payment Cap does not limit an increase in interest, but it does limit the size of your payment increase. For example, on an ARM with monthly payments of $700, a 7.5% Payment Cap would prevent your payment from exceeding $752.50 at the first adjustment, no matter how high the index has climbed. But watch out! If you are limiting the payment without limiting the interest rate, your payment may not be large enough to cover the interest that is due. The unpaid interest is not simply ignored, it's *deferred* — and added to your loan balance. This is also known as *negative amortization*. I recommend that you explore the other ARM options before choosing a loan with a balance that may *increase*.

CALCULATING ARM PAYMENTS

The initial monthly payments on an ARM loan are calculated in exactly the same way you would calculate payments for a fixed-rate loan. Since most ARMs have a 30-year term, use the factor in the amortization chart for 30-year loans at the note rate for your ARM. However each time the interest rate on your ARM is adjusted, the payments are recalculated and re-amortized over the remaining term.

For example, on a 1-year ARM, at the first adjustment, there will be 29 years remaining. To calculate the new payment amount with the amortization chart (see **Appendix I**, use the new interest rate, the *remaining* term (29 years), and the loan balance at that time.

CONVERTIBILITY TO A FIXED RATE

Many lenders offer ARM loans that may be converted to fixed-rate loans at a later date. This provision is not free; to obtain a convertible ARM, you may have to pay a slightly higher interest rate — usually one-eighth to one-half a percentage point higher than the rate for an ordinary ARM. The question is, should you? While convertibility is a feature most borrowers consider important, it is estimated that fewer than 10% of them actually exercise the conversion option. The reason is purely a monetary one. When you convert your ARM to a fixed-rate loan, your interest rate will be increased to match the current market rate for fixed-rate loans. That could easily be an increase of 3% — a jump that would result in significantly higher payments.

These higher payments make sense only if interest rates are on the rise. Increasing index rates could push the payments on ARM loans well beyond your new fixed rate. But if rates should stay the same or drop, you would save money with your ARM. So it's a gamble, and most borrowers choose convertible ARMs simply to leave their options open. They may want to do some gambling later on.

Although many ARM loans are convertible only at certain specified dates, some of today's ARMs may be converted to fixed-rate loans anytime after the first month. If you decide to convert your ARM, you'll be charged a fee at the time of conversion, although it will be less than the cost of refinancing a non-convertible ARM to a new fixed-rate loan. As you evaluate this loan, compare two things: the cost of the higher interest rate on a convertible ARM plus the fee to convert versus the cost of refinancing a non-convertible ARM.

WHICH INDEX IS BEST?

Even after plenty of research, I can't answer that question. All the indexes fluctuate in concert with the economic climate. But they all react to that climate with slightly different characteristics. Some respond quickly to changes; others are slow to react.

Lenders frequently offer several different loans, based on different indexes. Some indexes are familiar to borrowers; others are strange and unknown tongue-twisters. How would you like to come face-to-face with this one: 'the Federal Home Loan Mortgage Corporation posted yield requirement for 60-day delivery of fixed-rate 30-year loans plus 50 basis points index'? That name's enough to make even stout-hearted borrowers run the other direction.

To evaluate an index, ask your loan officer for more information about its volatility. Charts are available which show how different indexes have moved in past years. With these in hand, you'll be able to note differences that will affect the interest rate on your ARM.

WHO SHOULD CHOOSE AN ARM?

Some borrowers turn to ARM loans for reasons of affordability. With the ARM's lower interest rates and correspondingly low payments, borrowers can qualify for a much larger ARM than a fixed-rate loan. But even if you can easily afford any loan, there are times when it makes very good economic sense to choose an ARM.

Borrowers who are planning to stay in a home only a few years can often save plenty of interest by choosing an ARM over a fixed-rate loan. Lenders occasionally indulge in a modified price war with their ARM loans, offering them at enticingly low note rates, knowing that the rates can be increased upon adjustment. If you are tempted by a low 'teaser' rate, be sure to ask your loan officer if there is negative amortization (deferred interest) with this loan. Will your attractively low starting payments actually cover all the interest that is due? In past years, some ARMs have had deferred interest, although these loans are not as commonly available as they once were. Still, it's wise to check.

ADVANTAGES OF AN ARM

1. Lower interest rate (at least initially) than that for a fixed-rate loan.

2. Lower monthly payments, initially.

3. Lower income needed to qualify.

4. Advantageous if interest rates later drop.

DISADVANTAGES OF AN ARM

1. Unpredictability of interest rates.

2. Unpredictability of monthly payments.

NEWFANGLED IDEAS

Two new loans have been gaining popularity recently: the 5- or 10-year ARM, and the biweekly payment loan. Both meet special needs of homebuyers and are certainly worth researching.

THE 5- 0R 10-YEAR ARM

Definition: **A 5- or 10-year ARM has an interest rate that remains fixed for the original adjustment period, then is adjusted on a yearly basis for the remaining term of the loan.**

When is an ARM not an ARM? When it's sitting squarely on the fence between adjustable and fixed rates. Here is an ARM that masquerades as a fixed-rate loan for its first adjustment period, then becomes a traditional 1-year ARM for its remaining term. Since most homeowners move within five or six years, this is an excellent loan for borrowers who want to combine some of the advantages of both fixed- and adjustable-rate financing.

With the 5- or 10-year ARM (and with a similar 3-year ARM that's also available), buyers can enjoy a lower interest rate than that for a fixed-rate loan, although probably not as low as the rate on a traditional 1-year ARM. Then, too, they'll have the stability and predictability of payments and interest rate for several years.

THE BIWEEKLY PAYMENT LOAN

Definition: **A biweekly payment loan has a two-week (rather than monthly) payment schedule, requiring the borrower to make 26 payments per year.**

Who wants to make 26 payments a year instead of 12? Plenty of borrowers think it's a great idea! With the biweekly loan, a borrower pays approximately half a standard monthly payment every two weeks. Simple arithmetic shows that these 26 biweekly payments add up to the equivalent of 13 monthly payments in each year. Like the 15-year fixed-rate loan, the biweekly loan builds equity faster than a standard 30-year loan, since the borrower is making extra payments. Consequently, it is repaid faster than its standard counterpart.

The disadvantages of this loan are similar to those of the 15-year fixed-rate loan: it is more difficult to qualify for, and the rapid equity build-up can be a drawback if you should need to sell your home in a slow market. Because the biweekly payments add extra paperwork for the lending institution each month, many lenders insist that an automatic-payment checking or savings account be set up, to pay the lender directly. Consider, instead, choosing a standard fixed-rate loan, but making an extra monthly payment per year, with your lender's permission.

BUYDOWNS INCREASE AFFORDABILITY

Definition: **A buydown is a sum of money advanced to the lender at time of closing, in exchange for a reduction in the interest rate of the loan. In effect, a buydown is a form of prepaid interest.**

Affordability is often high priority when it comes to choosing a loan. Many buyers find it difficult — or impossible — to obtain a loan that's large enough to buy the home they've set their sights on. Enter, the **buydown,** a handy little financing technique that makes almost any loan more affordable.

A buydown performs its miracles by reducing the interest rate on your loan. As you've discovered, a lower interest rate will lower the required monthly payments, and the lower payments will, in turn, make qualifying easier. For example, on a $50,000 30-year loan with an interest rate of 11%, you'd need over $3700 *more income* to qualify than for a similar loan at 9%. With a buydown, you'll be able to obtain a significantly larger loan without waiting for a raise in salary.

This kind of financial miracle is not free of charge. You'll be required to pay your lender a **buydown fee** at closing, when the final loan documents are signed. The amount of the fee will depend upon the type and size of buydown you choose. And here's the good news: the buydown fee does not have to be paid by the buyer. Sellers often pay buydown fees to help buyers qualify for a loan. If you'd like to ask the seller to pay, your request should be made as part of your written purchase offer.

TWO KINDS OF BUYDOWNS

A **permanent buydown** is one in which the interest rate remains at a constant low level for the entire term of the loan. A **temporary buydown**, in comparison, changes the interest rate only for a short time — just long enough to give a borrower an opportunity to qualify for the loan at the lower interest rate and to ease comfortably into higher payments. After that, the rate returns to its original pre-buydown level (or on an adjustable-rate loan, to the level it would have reached without the buydown).

PERMANENT BUYDOWNS

Permanent buydowns are not used as extensively as their temporary counterparts for two reasons: first, they're considerably more expensive, and secondly, they're not as effective a qualifying tool. Most borrowers use buydowns simply to qualify for a larger loan. Once they've qualified, they don't *need* reduced payments for thirty years.

You can determine the approximate cost of a permanent

66

buydown on a 30-year loan very easily. Simply estimate a fee of 6% of the loan amount for every 1% interest reduction. For example, on a $50,000 loan with an interest rate of 11%, it will cost 6% of $50,000 — or $3,000 — to reduce the interest to 10% for the full 30 years. Or a fee of $6,000 would reduce the interest to 9% for the term of the loan.

TEMPORARY BUYDOWNS

Temporary buydowns are stopgap measures; they usually remain in effect for only one to three years, but produce magnificent results while they last. Their primary purpose is to reduce the monthly payments so that the borrower can qualify for the loan.

While there are different ways to structure a temporary buydown, the most common variety you'll encounter is known as the **graduated buydown**. Here the interest rate is lowered substantially the first year, then raised gradually, until it matches the original interest rate of the loan. One popular graduated buydown is known as the 3-2-1 buydown. It reduces the interest rate on a loan 3% the first year, only 2% the second year (that's 2% below the original rate), and 1% the third. From the fourth year on, the interest remains at the pre-buydown rate. Here's how a 3-2-1 buydown would affect a $50,000 30-year fixed-rate loan at 11% interest:

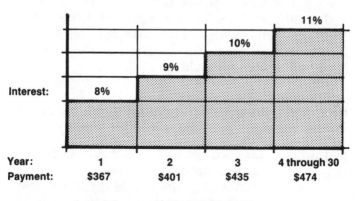

Year:	1	2	3	4 through 30
Payment:	$367	$401	$435	$474

HOW A 3-2-1 BUYDOWN WORKS

There are a number of different graduated buydowns, reducing the interest rate in differing amounts, over different terms. For example, a 2-1 buydown would last just two years, lowering the interest 2% the first year and only 1% the second. The following chart shows a variety of graduated buydowns and a formula for calculating their cost.

Cost Of A Graduated Buydown

Type of Buydown	Estimated Buydown Fee
3-2-1	.055 X the amount of the loan
3-3-1	.064 X the amount of the loan
3-1-1	.046 X the amount of the loan
3-1	.037 X the amount of the loan
2-2-1	.046 X the amount of the loan
2-1-1	.037 X the amount of the loan
2-1	.028 X the amount of the loan

Using the chart, you can calculate the cost of a 3-2-1 buydown on a $50,000 loan:

$$\$50,000 \times .055 = \$2,750$$

BUYDOWNS ON ALL TYPES OF LOANS

Buydowns are available for many different kinds of loans, for adjustable as well as fixed-rate, for 15-year as well as 30-year financing. But not every lender offers every type of buydown on every loan; ask your loan officer to explain which buydowns are available on the loans you've been researching.

DISCOUNT POINTS: BUYDOWNS INCOGNITO

Definition: Like a buydown, a discount point is a form of prepaid interest — paid to the lender at closing. One discount point costs one percent of the loan amount.

You may be old enough to remember a time when **discount points** had a bad reputation. But recently, discount points have taken on a whole new image. In the past, discount points — or **points**, as they are often called — were rarely used with conventional loans, but they were prominent in government financing. For some government loans a *seller*, even today, is required to pay a number of discount points. The cost, at a time when interest rates were fluctuating wildly, was unpredictable and often high. Today discount points on conventional loans are predictable and reasonable. Like buydowns, they add an element of affordability to home financing, but one that buyers often aren't aware of.

A discount point is a fee that is paid to the lender. One discount point equals one percent of the amount of the loan. So for a $50,000 loan, each discount point would cost $500. What borrowers don't often see is what that discount point is actually *buying*. As an example, take three different loans advertised by a lender: one is offered at 11% interest with no discount points; the second at 10½% interest with three discount points; and the third at 10% interest with six discount points. For a higher number of discount points paid, you'll receive a lower interest rate for the entire term of the loan. As you can see, discount points are simply permanent buydowns going by a different name.

Like buydowns, or other loan fees and closing costs, discount points may be paid by the buyer *or* seller. This may be an item you'd like to negotiate with the seller when you make your offer to purchase the home. Sellers who've had difficulty selling their homes are sometimes very willing to cooperate.

WATCH OUT FOR THESE LOANS!

There are some loans that should carry warning signs. As you've seen, many loans pose a high risk for lending institutions. However two loans carry a high element of risk for the *borrower*. These may be fine for some knowledgeable homebuyers, but I've seen many first-time buyers caught unawares. If you're shopping for financing, watch out for **Loans with Negative Amortization** and **Loans with Calls**.

Earlier in this chapter, you've seen how negative amortization — deferred interest — occurs when your payment is not large enough to cover the amount of interest that is due. The unpaid interest will be added to the loan balance, increasing the amount you owe. Negative amortization is found on some adjustable-rate loans with unusually low introductory rates. To be sure, ask your loan officer if the loan you're considering has any deferred interest.

LOANS WITH CALLS

Definition: Loans which give the lender the right to 'call' the loan (demand payment in full) on a specified date.

A **call provision** on a loan is sometimes referred to as a **balloon**. It requires you to repay the loan early, and to do so, you may be forced to either refinance your home or sell it.

This doesn't sound risky at first. You'll get a 30-year loan, at an attractively low interest rate, but with a five-year call provision (or sometimes a three- or ten-year call). "No problem," you decide. "I'll just refinance — or maybe set aside enough to pay the whole loan off." What's wrong? Take a look at a sample loan (a $50,000 30-year fixed-rate loan at 10% interest):

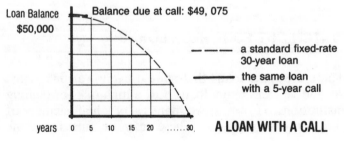

A LOAN WITH A CALL

Did you notice the loan balance after five years? On a $50,000 loan, it's still over $49,000! Be aware that financing (and refinancing) a loan is expensive. Loan fees and other costs can add up to several thousands of dollars. Consider this possibility, too: at the time your loan is called, what will the financing market be like? Will interest rates be so high that you won't be able to qualify for a new loan? And if the real estate market is sluggish, will you be able to sell your home to repay the loan? Think twice before putting yourself in a risky position.

RESEARCHING GOVERNMENT LOANS

Definition: **A Government Loan is one that is either insured, guaranteed or funded by a branch of the Federal, State or Local Government.**

In this book, I've placed government loans *after* the section on conventional financing for a very good reason. The types of loans that you'll discover in the private sector are all available in government financing, too. Once you've read about fixed- and adjustable-rate loans, 15- and 30-year terms, buydowns, discount points, mortgage insurance, plus all the other facts and facets of financing, you'll be able to see the advantages and disadvantages of government loans.

But just because government loans are in 'second place' in this book doesn't mean that you should ignore them in the early stages of your financing research. In fact, I recommend that buyers *start* their search by looking at government loans, to see what they have to offer. You'll find several advantages: some government loans (including the three Federal government programs we'll look at next) are available to borrowers with little or no down payment. Government loans often have lower loan fees and sometimes lower interest rates than conventional financing. This may make them easier to qualify for. So start by examining the following programs, then ask your real estate agent what loans, if any, are available from your state and local governments.

HUD/FHA LOANS

FHA (Federal Housing Administration) financing is the product of the most popular and wide-reaching government loan program in the United States today. Yet neither FHA nor HUD (the Department of Housing and Urban Development, under which FHA operates) is actually a lender. Instead, FHA provides a mortgage insurance program for institutional lenders who offer loans according to FHA specifications. With FHA to protect them against borrower default, these lenders are willing and able to make loans they would normally consider too risky — loans with a higher LTV ratio, lower loan fees and attractive interest rates.

The National Housing Act created the Federal Housing Administration in 1934 to improve conditions in the nation's mid-depression housing industry. Since that time, it has played an exceptionally innovative role in the real estate loan market. Widespread use of the amortized loan, better home construction methods and the standardization of appraisal techniques are just a few of the results FHA has achieved over the past fifty years.

WHO IS ELIGIBLE FOR AN FHA LOAN

Unlike other government loan programs, FHA does not have rigid eligibility requirements for most of its loans. Even wealthy borrowers may obtain FHA loans; they are available to any person who is a good credit risk and financially able to repay. Some FHA loans, however, are designed to meet the needs of special interest groups, such as veterans, or even condominium buyers! Low-income borrowers may qualify for a special FHA loan with payments subsidized by the Federal government. The overall range of FHA loans is very extensive.

Limits are set, though, on the *size* of loan you may obtain. This varies throughout the country, depending upon local housing prices. Currently the maximum loan amount available for a single-family home is $101,250, although the limit in your area may be lower.

FHA FINANCING INFORMATION

Since FHA *insures* rather than *lends*, you'll have to go elsewhere for your FHA loan — to an institutional lender, such as a bank, saving and loan association, mortgage company or mortgage broker. Not all lending institutions offer FHA loans, but many do. Here's your chance to compare the benefits of conventional versus FHA financing with one visit to a loan officer!

All FHA loans must carry mortgage insurance. Buyers with large down payments aren't given preferential treatment here, and so may find conventional financing more to their liking. For most FHA loans, the mortgage insurance payment is known as a **One-Time MIP**, although it may be paid in two ways: the entire cost may be paid in cash at closing or added to the loan balance.

There are discount points charged on most FHA loans, although it *is* possible to obtain an FHA loan without points by paying a slightly higher interest rate. As in conventional financing, discount points may be paid by either the buyer or the seller.

AND THE GOOD NEWS...

FHA loans are excellent for buyers with a small down payment. On the most popular type of FHA loan, known as the '203b', buyers may borrow up to 97% of the first $25,000 of the home's value, plus 95% of the remainder above $25,000. That means a home valued at $70,000 can be purchased with a down payment of only $3,000. (On conventional loans, a down payment of at least $3,500 would be needed.) And for homes valued at $50,000 or less, the loan-to-value ratio on most FHA loans is 97%!

A very attractive feature of FHA loans has been their *assumability*. Recently, stricter limits have been set on blind assumptions, as you'll read in the next chapter, but even so, the assumability of these loans is an important point to consider when you're choosing financing.

VETERANS ADMINISTRATION LOANS

Here's another Federal government program that has helped many prospective buyers finance a home: the VA loan program, offered by the Veterans Administration. These are loans designed for veterans who have served in the armed forces at some time since 1940. There are exceptions, though: individuals who've served in other organizations, programs or schools may qualify, as may spouses of prisoners of war, or of those missing or killed in action. Your nearest Veterans Administration office can help determine if you are eligible.

Like HUD, the Veterans Administration does not provide the funds for VA loans. These are offered by conventional lending institutions — usually the same lenders handling FHA loans. And like FHA and conventional financing, VA loans come in many of the standard varieties you've read about in this chapter.

Here is a loan that sounds too good to be true. The amazing thing about VA loans is their loan-to-value ratio: up to 100%! That's *no* down payment! And as an added bonus, there's no mortgage insurance with VA loans. Unlike the FHA program which offers insurance to the lender, the Veterans Administration *guarantees* that the lender will be reimbursed for certain losses if the borrower defaults and foreclosure is necessary. To cover the cost of the guaranty, VA does charge the buyer a **Funding Fee**, but it costs considerably less than mortgage insurance.

There is a maximum limit on the VA loan amount, but it is a more generous limit than that of FHA. Currently it is possible to obtain a 100% LTV VA loan up to $144,000, or loans in higher amounts with certain specified down payments.

Discount points are a part of VA financing, but here the seller *must* pay the basic number of points charged. (Buyers may pay additional points if they'd like a lower interest rate.)

FINANCING INFORMATION SHEET

Date: _____

Lender: _____

Address: _____

_____

Phone: _____

Loan Officer: _____

Loan amount requested: _____ LTV: _____

Type of loan: ☐ Conventional,   ☐ Government;

_____

Interest Rate: ____%, ☐ Fixed, ☐ Adjustable, ad-
  justs how often _____

For adjustable rate mortgages:
  Lifetime cap: _____%
  Adjustable cap: _____%
  Payment cap: _____%
  Index: _____
  Margin: _____
  Term: _____ years

Payment schedule: ☐ monthly, ☐ every 2 weeks

Estimated payments: $ _____, include:
  ☐ principal, ☐ interest, ☐ property tax reserves,
  ☐ homeowner's insurance reserves, ☐ mortgage
  insurance

Mortgage insurance: premium at closing
  $_____, monthly premium $_____

Discount points: $_____

Loan fee: $_____

Buydown information: _____

_____

_____

Gross monthly income needed to qualify: $_____

Estimated closing costs: $_____

  and downpayment: $_____

Estimated cash needed at closing: $_____

Notes: _____

_____

FARMERS HOME ADMINISTRATION LOANS

The Farmers Home Administration, another agency of the Federal government, offers what are known as FmHA loans to low-income borrowers who want to buy a modest home in a designated rural area. If you are eligible for another type of loan, or if your idea of a *modest* home includes a hot tub and skylights, the FmHA is not for you. These subsidized loans are available only to borrowers who cannot qualify for other financing. To apply for an FmHA loan, visit your regional office of the Farmers Home Administration. These loans are not available through conventional lenders.

OTHER GOVERNMENT LOANS

There may be other types of financing offered by your particular state or local government. For example, some states have loan programs for veterans, and you'll often find programs for moderate- or low-income borrowers, especially those who want to buy their first home. The best way to find out what is available in your area is to ask your real estate agent.

ORGANIZING YOUR RESEARCH

Now that you've studied this chapter, a visit to a loan officer will supply you with facts about specific loans that are being offered. Copy and use the **FINANCING INFORMATION WORKSHEET** included in this chapter to help you record your loan data, so that you'll be able to compare a variety of financing methods at a glance.

But new loans aren't for everyone — or for every home. There are times when economic necessity or just plain common sense rules out this possibility. That's when it's a good idea to have a stockpile of creative financing techniques ready. As you'll discover in **STEP SIX**, there are alternate ways to finance your first home.

76

STEP SIX

DISCOVER OTHER WAYS TO FINANCE A HOME

"Let us all be happy and live within our means, even if we have to borrer the money to do it with."

Artemis Ward

It's not always possible to get a new loan. You may not be able to qualify for a large enough loan to finance the home you want to buy. Then, too, the home you're buying may not qualify. Lenders will finance only those homes that are in remarkably healthy condition; if yours doesn't meet their requirements, you may need an alternate method of financing.

So it's not always *possible* to get a new loan. But it's not always *wise* to get one either. For instance, if interest rates on new loans are high, an alternate financing method may be a better choice. This chapter covers a variety of techniques that may come in handy when you're ready to buy your first home. We'll take a look at **assumptions, seller financing,** and that delightfully candid term, **sweat equity.** While you may not need these alternative financing techniques, it's a good idea to know what your available options are, before you make an offer on a home.

ASSUMING A LOAN

Imagine this: the home you'd like to buy is currently financed by a loan with a very low interest rate — much

77

lower than the current rates for new loans. You'd like to step into the seller's shoes and take over those attractively low payments. Sometimes that's possible; it's what's known as **assuming the loan,** or **an assumption**.

There's just one small hitch: while assumptions are not uncommon, *good* assumptions are hard to find. If you can latch onto a good assumption, however, it's a splendid way to finance a home. So just what is a good assumption? We'll look at two different types of assumptions and you'll soon see how to evaluate their potential for financing your home.

BLIND ASSUMPTIONS

Buyers love blind assumptions. With a **blind assumption** (or **simple assumption** as it's also called), the buyer may take over the seller's loan with exactly the same provisions (interest rate, term, etc.) that the seller has enjoyed. If the seller has made monthly payments of $423, at an interest rate of 7%, then you, the buyer, will continue to make the same payments, at the same rate of interest. This type of assumption is so simple that the lender will not even ask your name (let alone any other personal data) until *after* you have signed the final documents to purchase your home. The lender is turning a blind eye toward the transaction — hence the name, blind assumption.

The reason the lender is willing to do this centers around the idea of *release of liability*. With blind assumptions, sellers retain some liability for the loan, even after you purchase the home. If you, the purchaser, should default on the loan, the seller can be held liable to some extent.

QUALIFYING ASSUMPTIONS

The second type of assumption often lets the seller off the hook, but makes things a little more difficult for the buyer. With this type of assumption, you, the buyer, will have to qualify for the assumed loan, just as if you were applying for a new loan. The interest rate of the assumed loan is not certain to remain the same; in fact, the lender usually has the right to raise the interest rate upon assumption. Since you have qualified to take over this loan, the lender will, in most cases, give the seller a release of liability. Fees for qualifying assumptions are usually higher than those for blind assumptions, although assumption fees for either type are usually — but not always — lower than the fees for a new loan. As you can see, qualifying assumptions are not as attractive to buyers as blind assumptions. But when interest rates on new loans are high, even qualifying assumptions can be appealing if the assumed interest rate remains lower than that of a new loan.

FINDING A GOOD ASSUMPTION

So most buyers prefer to look for blind assumptions. The problem is this: they're becoming increasingly scarce. There was a time when many conventional loans, plus all FHA and VA loans, could be assumed via a blind assumption, but that is no longer the case. Most, if not all, conventional loans today are assumable only by the second method: the buyer must qualify and the interest rate may be increased. However some government loans still allow blind assumptions, although even there, the rules are becoming more restrictive.

FHA and VA loans have, in the past, been very attractive to assume. If the seller was willing to allow a blind assumption, then any FHA or VA loan could be assumed without qualifying. On FHA loans made before December 1, 1986, this is still the case. For more recent loans, FHA requires that buyers qualify if the loan is assumed within the first year of its term (or two years for loans made to investors). The seller and the buyer will remain jointly liable for five years, at which time the seller will be released of liability. VA loans made before February 1, 1988 may be assumed without qualifying if the seller permits a blind assumption. VA loans made since that time now require the buyer to qualify for an assumption.

As you can see, there *are* still good assumptions to be found. The best assumptions are those with a high loan balance and, of course, an attractive interest rate. Old loans often have excellent rates but their loan balances have decreased considerably. Inflation has no doubt increased the value of the home, too, widening the gap between the loan balance and the sales price. This gap — the seller's equity — must be paid or financed in some way. How you decide fill the gap will often determine whether the assumption is a practical financing method for that particular home.

A SECOND MORTGAGE TO FILL THE GAP

If your down payment isn't large enough to repay the seller's equity, you may consider a **second mortgage loan**. Second mortgages are those added after the first mortgage is in place. For example, a home improvement or equity loan would be a second mortgage loan if the home is already financed by another loan. A second mortgage loan is riskier for a lender than a first mortgage loan for this reason: if the buyer should default and the property is sold at a foreclosure sale, the proceeds will be used first to repay the first mortgage lender. Any additional funds will go to the second mortgage lender — then the third mortgage lender and so on. Since foreclosure often brings very meager returns, the second mortgage holder runs the risk of not being repaid in full.

That is why second mortgage loans from institutional lenders are usually offered with higher interest rates, shorter terms and lower LTVs than those for first mortgage loans. Second mortgage loans *can* be expensive. If you're considering an assumption, calculate the whole package: the cost of both the assumption and the second mortgage loan. Weigh this against the cost of a new first mortgage loan or other financing to see if it stacks up favorably.

Sellers often provide second mortgage financing, too. Instead of paying the sellers for their equity at closing, consider asking them (in your offer to purchase the home) to carry a second mortgage for part (or all) of their equity. You'll work out an agreement with the seller to pay for the equity over a period of time, rather than in one lump-sum payment at closing. Since sellers are not bound by institutional lending rules, you may be able to negotiate an interest rate, LTV and payment schedule that are far more appealing than those on institutional 'seconds'.

If you do decide to finance the home by means of a qualifying assumption plus any second mortgage loan (from a lending institution or the seller), the sum of both payments will be used to qualify you for the assumption.

SELLER FINANCING: THE CONTRACT

Sellers often finance more than just a second mortgage; frequently they act as the *only* lender involved in a transaction. One form of seller financing that has long been popular is the **contract**. It's known, in different parts of the country, as a **land sales contract**, **land contract**, **contract for deed** or **installment contract**.

A contract is an agreement between the buyer and the seller. To illustrate the procedure of *buying on contract*, let's take, as an example, a $60,000 home that the sellers have financed by a $25,000 loan. (That means the sellers' equity is $35,000.) The prospective buyers have a down payment of $10,000. What are their financing options?

- They could obtain a new loan in the amount of $50,000. At closing, the sellers' original loan ($25,000) would be repaid and the sellers would receive $35,000, as payment for their equity.

- The buyers could assume the sellers' $25,000 loan, the sellers would receive $10,000 as payment for part of their equity, and the remaining $25,000 could be financed with a second mortgage loan. (If an institutional second is obtained, the sellers would receive payment for their entire equity.)

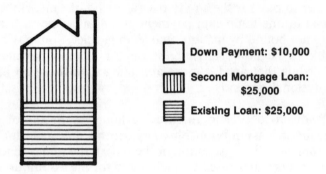

Down Payment: $10,000

Second Mortgage Loan: $25,000

Existing Loan: $25,000

AN ASSUMPTION PLUS SECOND

- The sellers would keep their existing loan, but enter into a contract with the buyers for the amount of $50,000 (the sales price minus the down payment). The sellers would receive the $10,000 down payment at closing, as payment for part of their equity. They would receive monthly payments from the buyers and they, the sellers, would continue to make monthly payments to their original lender.

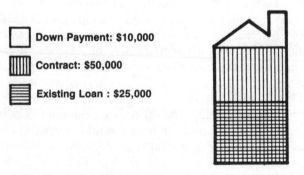

Down Payment: $10,000

Contract: $50,000

Existing Loan : $25,000

A CONTRACT SALE

One way a contract sale differs from the other two methods is that the seller's existing loan (if any) remains intact. It is neither assumed nor repaid. The seller will continue to make the monthly payments on that loan, usually out of the larger payment received from the buyer. The remainder of the buyer's payment will be kept by the seller, as payment for the equity.

How and *when* the buyer pays the seller — whether monthly, bi-weekly or even yearly — is a matter for negotiation between the two parties. That's the beauty of a contract: the exact details may be anything that is agreed upon by both buyer and seller, within legal limits, of course. The rules that the institutional lenders use simply don't apply here. Buyers who cannot qualify for an institutional loan can often buy a home on contract; sellers are sometimes quite willing to bend the traditional qualification standards if they feel assured that the buyers are reliable.

If there is an existing loan, that lender *may* wish to approve the contract and the buyer before allowing the sale to take place. *Never* enter into a contract sale without first receiving written permission from the seller's lender. Lenders often have the right to call the loan (insist that it be paid in full immediately) if the home is sold on contract without the lender's knowledge.

WHEN THE HOME CAN'T QUALIFY

Often *homes* fail to pass the institutional lenders' scrutiny, too. These homes are prime candidates for a contract sale. If you're willing to buy a less-than-perfect property, seller financing is an excellent way to do it. But beware of major problems that cannot be solved easily. A home without a complete foundation is a good example. If lenders will not finance such a home and you to buy it on contract, you'll have a non-financeable home when *you* decide to sell. That will reduce your chances of receiving cash for your equity. You'll have to sell on contract also, unless you have improved the foundation to the lenders' standards in the meantime.

CONSULT AN ATTORNEY

If you are buying on contract, be sure to ask an attorney to prepare or review the contract before you sign it. I have seen so many difficulties grow out of contract sales that could have been avoided with legal advice. On the other hand, I've seen contract sales that have been the very best possible way to finance a particular home.

Your attorney can give suggestions of provisions you may wish to have included in your contract. For instance, you may want a contract that can be assumed by a new buyer when you decide to sell the home. You may want small monthly payments for the first few years, with larger payments later. Or perhaps you'd like interest-only payments for awhile. That's why seller financing is a good example of what's popularly called *creative financing*. There are very few limits to the creative terms you and the seller can devise!

BE CAREFUL OF BALLOONS!

One provision that is often seen in contracts is the **balloon payment**, similar to a call provision in a loan. At a certain specified time, the entire remaining contract balance must be paid in full. Watch out! Reread the section in **STEP FIVE** that covers **Loans With Calls** before you enter into a risky agreement.

In general, consider buying a home on contract if you or the home you are buying cannot qualify for a new institutional loan. This is a good method to try also, when interest rates are unappealingly high; sellers are often willing to offer a better rate and terms than you'd find elsewhere.

HANDY? TRY SWEAT EQUITY

Handy with a hammer? Here's a financing technique that will help you trade elbow grease for a down payment. It's known as **sweat equity** and it has proved to be a way for many buyers with little or no down payment to buy a home of their own. With sweat equity, a buyer can receive credit towards the purchase price by working to repair the home. So if you're looking for a **fixer-upper** — a home that's in need of repair — sweat equity may be just what you need.

Sweat equity may be used with seller financing or with a new institutional or government loan. Either way, you should seek the advice and assistance of an attorney. I like to call sweat equity 'Blood, Sweat and Tears Equity', since it can be the breeding ground for some potentially outstanding real estate catastrophes.

Here's just a hint of what might happen: problems start when you try to determine what repairs should 'count' toward your down payment, or what value should be given to the work you're going to do. Who pays for the materials? What quality of materials will be used? And what happens if the buyer knocks down a wall, only to find termites kicking up their heels between the studs? Problems with sweat equity can be considerable. That is why good legal advice is essential. Ask your attorney to draw up an agreement between you and the seller, to avoid problems that may crop up later.

If you want to use sweat equity with a new loan, talk to your loan officer before you enter into any agreement with the seller. Each lender has different rules as to what work may or may not be counted as part of your down payment. Some lenders refuse to allow sweat equity at all. Many insist that buyers have a minimum down payment in cash, before using sweat equity as extra down payment, to improve their loan-to-value ratio. Most lenders will require an appraisal to determine what repairs are needed. Usually only essential repairs will count as sweat equity if you are getting a new loan.

However with seller financing, you and the seller may agree to count any work you'd like as part of your down payment.

Assumptions, seller financing and sweat equity are all excellent techniques that give you additonal financing options beyond the realm of new loans. Keep all of these in mind as you continue your house-hunting and, in **STEP SEVEN**, make an offer to buy your first home.

STEP SEVEN

MAKE AN OFFER TO BUY A HOME

"If there were dreams to sell, what would you buy?"   *Thomas Lovell Beddoes*

Whew! After plenty of investigative research, you've come to Step Seven. By this time, you've mastered the skills you'll need to make a choice. You've selected a Target Area and become an expert on homes, both *for sale* and *sold*, in that neighborhood. At the same time, you began your research into the many financing methods available to you. You know what you can comfortably afford, and you've been actively looking for the perfect first home. The next step is to figure out what to do when you find it.

CALL IN THE PROFESSIONALS

Once you've found the home you'd like to buy, it's time to give it a final evaluation before you make an offer. While my purpose in writing this book is to make you feel confident enough to conquer the real estate market, I'm going to add a word of caution. **Ask for expert advice.** Buying a home is a major investment and, like many other major investments, it's not risk-free.

I had bought and sold a number of properties before I decided to study real estate law and financing. What I learned very quickly was that I had been exceptionally lucky. Somehow I had managed to miss the really serious problems that often occur. Since then, I've seen many disastrous real estate transactions that could have been avoided with professional help.

Most buyers are not sufficiently knowledgeable to pinpoint serious hidden physical defects. Most real estate agents aren't either. But there are companies or individuals who conduct complete home inspections. For a fee, they'll give you a thorough evaluation of a home's condition — inside, outside, and in all the nooks and crannies where you probably wouldn't want to venture. Then there are firms that specialize in one area of expertise: termite and dry rot inspections, or electrical or roofing evaluations, for example. An inspection may cost $50 or $200, or sometimes more. But compared to the cost of buying a home with an expensive defect, even $200 is very little to pay for peace of mind.

However $100 or $200 is a hefty sum to plunk down on a house you may not eventually buy. Multiply that by two or three different homes, and you'll find your cash reserves dwindling at an alarming rate. So here's how to handle the inspection situation.

When you find the home you'd like to buy, look at it with your most critical eye. Spend plenty of time for a close evaluation. After careful scrutiny, you may uncover some problem areas. But your real goal, instead, should not be to find all the defects, but simply to determine what kind of professional inspection, if any, would be best suited to this particular home.

I usually suggest that buyers *not* have an inspection made before submitting an offer to buy the home, unless they feel completely unable to formulate an offer without full details in hand. Instead, I recommend that an offer to purchase be written *contingent upon the the buyer's approval of the inspection results*. That means simply that the inspection will be made only after your offer has been accepted by the seller. If the results of the inspection do not meet with your approval, you will not be bound by the offer. You'll be free to submit a different (perhaps lower) offer or consider other homes instead. This way, you will not have to spend money for an inspection until you know that the terms and price you have offered are acceptable to the seller.

WHO PAYS FOR THE INSPECTION?

If the buyer wants an inspection made, then it usually is the buyer's responsibility to pay for it. However real estate practices vary somewhat throughout the U.S. In some parts of the country, sellers are routinely asked to provide certificates showing the absence of termites. That means that the sellers must have a termite inspection made at their expense. However in other states, buyers are expected to pay. Your real estate agent can tell you what is customary in your area. Even if tradition dictates that you, the buyer, should pay for an inspection, you may ask the seller to pay instead. Some sellers are very willing to do so in order to get their home sold. This request should be made in writing as part of your offer to purchase, as you'll see later in this chapter.

TYPES OF INSPECTIONS TO CONSIDER

New Construction Evaluation:
If the home is new, your concerns will center upon the quality of construction; dry rot and termites will not have had time to move in. While you could ask an independent inspection firm to give you an assessment, one of the best (and least expensive) ways to determine quality is to talk to the owners of other similar homes built by the same contractor. If you find recurring problems in the other homes, problems such as leaks or settling, for example, you'll have an idea of what to look for in the home you're considering.

For new homes or recently constructed homes, you'll want to inquire about any warranty that is in effect, providing protection against construction defects. One of the most widely offered is the HOW, or Home Owners

Warranty, which covers a broad range of defects for the first two years, plus an additional eight years of protection against major structural problems. This particular warranty is passed from owner to owner within that ten-year period, so many 'young' homes are still covered. Since a builder must pay a fee to obtain a HOW warranty, many contractors prefer to offer their own warranty program. Evaluate such warranties carefully. While many reputable builders provide good, sound coverage, other warranties are less dependable. Ask your real estate agent to obtain detailed information about the warranty offered.

General Home Inspection:
If the home is not newly built, you have a wider range of problems to choose from! An overall inspection of the home's condition becomes increasingly important with older houses. Your real estate agent may be able to give you the names of firms in your area that offer such a service, or you'll often find advertisements for home inspection companies in the newspaper housing ads or telephone directory. Before you hire an inspector, be sure you know exactly what you are getting. What service can you expect? Ask these questions before signing an inspection contract:

- What parts of the home will be checked? (*Attic? Basement? Crawl space? Exterior as well as interior? Foundation? Roof? Insulation? Electrical, gas and plumbing systems? Built-in appliances?*)
- What defects will the inspector specifically look for?
- Will the inspection cover infestation and damage by wood-destroying organisms such as termites and dry rot?
- What guarantee, if any, is offered?
- Are any defects, conditions, or parts of the home excluded from the guarantee?

Wood-destroying Organisms Inspection:
In most parts of the U.S., termites and other wood-destroying organisms feel right at home. They can do extensive damage before it's visible to the prospective buyer. Therefore a wood-destroying organisms inspec-

tion is recommended throughout the country. The cost is usually very reasonable, and the inspection may uncover infestations of carpenter ants or serious dry rot as well. Even homes just a few years old fall prey to these problems, so most buyers should consider this a routine precaution. If you're having an overall home inspection done, this inspection may or may not be included. Be sure to ask!

Roof Inspection:
If the roof is showing signs of age, or if you see evidence of a leak on the ceiling inside, you would be well advised to have a professional inspection. Again, if you are hiring a firm to give a general whole-house inspection, this may be a part of that evaluation and a second inspection may not be necessary.

Electrical, Plumbing or Heating System Inspections:
These are usually requested when buyers suspect or know of defects. The general home inspection usually provides a cursory check of these systems to see that they are functioning, but for known problems, an additional inspection by a specialist is wise.

Other Inspections:
If, on your tour of the home, you notice any defects or potential problems — structural defects, for example — make a note to yourself to request an inspection when your offer is being written. Peace of mind is worth far more than most inspections cost!

GETTING READY TO MAKE AN OFFER

When your research is completed and you feel confident that you've assessed the condition of the home to the best of your ability, it's time to consider just what you'd like to offer the seller. An offer to purchase a home is a written legal document that contains many terms and conditions. Your real estate agent, or in some cases your attorney, will help you structure your offer and will write it for you. The document used is commonly known as an **Offer to Purchase** or a **Sales Agreement And Receipt for Earnest Money**.

Included in this document will be all the specific terms and conditions of your offer to purchase the home. Such things as the **offered price**, the amount of **earnest money** (you'll read more about that in a moment), the amount of your **down payment** and your method of **financing** the home will all be clearly defined. The offer will specify when your transaction will be completed (that's called the **closing**, or **settlement**, or **escrow**) and the date you wish to take **possession** of the home. You'll also be able to add to the offer any special requests you may have. For example, you may want to have certain items included in the purchase price — items such as appliances or draperies. And *this* is the time to request permission to obtain any inspections you feel are necessary.

Your offer should be specific in every detail. Problems often occur in real estate transactions through misunderstanding or poor communication. That's why it's important to have a complete offer that leaves nothing open to misinterpretation. If you're asking for permission to have a roof inspection, for instance, give all the particulars: when it will be conducted (on or before a certain date), who will pay for the inspection, and what effect, if any, will the results have on the offer (is the offer contingent upon your approval of the results?).

WHO SHOULD WRITE THE OFFER?

Because an offer becomes a binding agreement once it has been accepted by the seller, it is important for your original offer to be written with great care. This is not a project for the do-it-yourselfer who has little or no experience in real estate law. A competent real estate agent using a standard Sales Agreement form should have no difficulty in preparing a straightforward offer to purchase a home. Most offers *are* written by agents.

But if you still feel confused or uncertain about any part of the offer after your agent has explained it, ask your attorney to review it before you sign. In some parts of the U.S., real estate attorneys are more widely used than in others. Later in this book, in STEP NINE, you'll learn just *when* and *why* attorneys are sometimes essential in the final closing process.

WHAT'S A FAIR PRICE TO OFFER?

If you've done all the research I've suggested throughout the chapters of this book, I know you'll have a good idea of the fair market value of the home. But many buyers wonder if they should hire a professional appraiser. **Fee appraisals**, as they are called, are not inexpensive. While they vary in price from area to area, and from home to home, you will no doubt pay at least $175 (and often more) for a professional opinion. Most homes are easy enough to evaluate without the need for an appraisal, so appraisals are not often requested by residential buyers. But if you have serious doubts about the value of the property, that option is open to you.

Even if you are *absolutely certain* that you know the fair market value of a home, what price should you offer the seller? That may be quite a different matter. Should you start with a very low offer, and hope you can wangle a deal on the way up, somewhere between rock bottom and reasonable? Or should you forget the game-playing and write a take-it-or-leave-it-offer at the top price you're willing to pay?

Unfortunately there is no one magic answer to these questions. There are, however, some guidelines that will help you decide where your offer should start:

- **Determine what is common practice in your area.** In a community that's experiencing a seller's market — where homes are in demand — buyers who start with a very low offer may find themselves outbid by three or four other higher offers being presented at the same time. There are areas where the market is so 'hot', offers are written in excess of the asking price. On the other hand, where the real estate market is sluggish, a low offer will have a chance of success. Your agent can give you statistics that compare sales prices to final listing prices in your community.

- **Leave room for negotiation.** Consider your needs and capabilities first. How much can you afford to spend? How much are you willing to spend? Unless you are in neck-and-neck competition and are willing to pay full price, it's often a good idea to back down from your top limit and allow negotiating space between your offer and the listing price. Avoid 'take-it-or-leave-it' offers. It's been my experience that they usually get left, not taken. Or if they are accepted, the sellers (who feel somewhat cheated out of a say in the matter) will often be less cooperative in the final stages of the purchase.

- **Don't waste time with ridiculously unfair offers.** It's tempting to want to get a bargain price on a great piece of property. And there certainly are bargains around, especially when sellers are anxious to sell. But while I applaud the motto, "If you don't ask, the answer's No", I have found that it pays to be reasonable. *Unreasonably* low offers not only waste time, but often generate hostility. Recognize that many sellers *love* their home and become terribly insulted if your price is too low. They'll flatly refuse to deal, even if you later decide to submit a reasonable offer. Study the situation beforehand; find out how motivated the sellers are, and base your offer accordingly.

EARNEST MONEY: HOW EARNEST ARE YOU?

Earnest money is a small portion of your down payment that you present with your offer to show your good faith. You are indicating that you are earnest in your intent to purchase the home. But how can you put a price on 'earnestness'? How much earnest money should you offer?

The answer depends primarily upon two factors: the price of the home and local custom in your area. In some parts of the country, $100 may be thought of as sufficient earnest money for a modest home, while in other areas, sellers expect $500, $1,000, or more. In general, offers for higher-priced homes are accompanied by larger amounts of earnest money. Ask your real estate agent what is common in your community.

The purpose of earnest money is this: if you back out of your agreement to buy the home after the seller has accepted it, you may lose your right to reclaim the earnest money. The seller may receive it as compensation for taking the home off the market when your offer was accepted. There are certain circumstances in which your earnest money will be returned to you if you are not able to complete the sale. An example might be if you cannot obtain financing. However, these circumstances should be clearly outlined in your offer.

Earnest money is usually held in a neutral trust account by the real estate broker, an attorney or an escrow company. It should not be given to the seller until the transaction is completed and the final funds are being disbursed. Your offer should specify where the earnest money is to be held.

THE OFFER IS PRESENTED!

Once your offer has been written, and you've signed it, it is ready to be presented to the sellers or their agent. Who makes the actual presentation is again a matter of local custom. In some parts of the country, your agent will explain the offer to the sellers and their listing agent. In other areas, the listing agent will make the presentation. You'll be at home, anxiously waiting for the verdict!

In your offer, you will have given the sellers a limited time in which to respond. After the date and time given, your offer will be null and void. It is usually a good idea to give the sellers a reasonably short time to answer your offer. Often a day or two is sufficient. A longer time will increase the chance of another, competing offer being received.

During the allotted time, the sellers will do one of three things:

1. **They'll accept the offer in its entirety.** In that case, the offer has been agreed to by both parties and you have a binding contract.

2. **The sellers will reject your offer.** No agreement has been reached. You're back to square one: you are free to make a second offer on that home or on another property.

3. **The sellers will reject your offer and make a counter-offer.** In this case, they'll alter the terms of your offer and make an offer back to you. Once you receive a counter-offer from the sellers, it's your turn. You may either accept or reject it. If the counter-offer is acceptable to you in its entirety, then you and the seller have reached a binding agreement. But if the counter-offer is *not* acceptable to you, you may reject it and, if you wish, submit another offer. Or you are free to make an offer on another home. Negotiations will continue until an agreement has been reached or until an impasse occurs.

Once you have submitted an offer to the seller, you are bound by that offer *if* the seller accepts it within the given time. However, if the seller rejects your offer, makes a counter-offer, or allows the time to lapse without responding, you are not under a binding agreement.

When you and the seller have signed the offer, it's time to move on to **STEP EIGHT**... the Loan Application. If you are not obtaining a new loan or most types of assumption, you'll skip this step, and head right to **STEP NINE**, for the Closing.

STEP EIGHT

PREPARE FOR THE LOAN APPLICATION

"The human species, according to the best theory I can form of it, is composed of two distinct races, those who borrow and those who lend."

Charles Lamb

Unless you're financing your new home by means of a blind assumpton or seller financing, you'll have to pay an official visit to your lender for the purpose of applying for your new loan. This is what's known as the **Loan Application,** or in lending jargon, the **Loan App.**

Most new loans are processed by banks, savings and loan associations, thrifts, mortgage companies, mortgage brokers or credit unions. These lending institutions take applications not only for conventional financing but also for many types of government loans, such as the FHA and VA programs. Not every lender handles all types of loans, so be sure to choose one that services the particular program you have in mind.

HOW TO CHOOSE A "GOOD" LENDER

Lending institutions are kept in check by governmental regulations and common-sense banking practices. As a result, there is great similarity between them in the mechanics of loan processing. That does not, however, mean that all lending institutions are equal. They differ in the types of loans offered, as well as interest rates and other specific terms of each loan. Keep in mind that loan officers aren't created equal either. A competent, conscientious loan officer can see that your paperwork is processed quickly and efficiently. So choose a loan officer with a good track record. Word-of-mouth recommendations are valuable; ask your real estate agent for advice before making a decision.

With so many different kinds of lending institutions, it's natural to wonder what *type* of institution would give you the best service or the lowest interest. Is it better to go to a savings and loan association specializing in home loans, or would you receive better terms from a bank or a mortgage company? Unfortunately there is no easy way to group lending institutions according to their level or quality of service. Each type of lending institution — bank, savings and loan association, credit union, mortgage company or mortgage broker — offers excellent loans and service for homebuyers. The differences lie in the individual institutions, their loans and their loan officers.

Buyers often wonder, too, whether they'd receive preferential treatment from the bank where they have their checking and saving accounts. While it may feel less intimidating to seek financing in familiar surroundings, familiarity is not a valid economic reason for choosing a lender. In most cases, lenders cannot and will not make concessions that are financially attractive simply because you are a loyal customer. Lending institutions today are not like the local banks of years past. They are, by necessity, dependent upon an outside support system and as a result, are not able to establish their own guidelines in the matter of loans.

WHO WRITES THE LENDING RULES?

Another name for this section of the book might be **Why You Can't Argue With A Loan Officer — And Win!**

Lenders are bound by certain guidelines when making loans and if you understand where these rules originate, you'll know what your chances are, if any, for stretching the guidelines to meet your needs.

Three of the most powerful rule-makers in the banking industry are affectionately known as **Fannie Mae, Freddie Mac** and **Ginnie Mae**. These three, properly named the Federal National Mortgage Association (FNMA), the Federal Home Loan Mortgage Corporation (FHLMC), and the Government National Mortgage Association (GNMA) respectively, are agencies which buy loans from lending institutions. This is what is known as the **secondary market**.

Lenders sell their loans at a discount to investors on the secondary market. The cash proceeds from the sale can, in turn, be used to finance other loans. An institution which is unable to sell its loans to investors will be limited in its ability to service the market, since lenders cannot continue to make loans without available funds. Fannie Mae, Ginnie Mae and Freddie Mac are three of the major investors in home mortgage loans. Insurance companies also buy heavily on the secondary market. Loans are sold in blocks, or groups worth millions of dollars, and so the investors are usually large corporations or syndicates of individual investors.

Investors are fussy about the loans they buy. Since they intend to make a profit from their purchases, they like to keep a careful eye on the risks. Each investor issues a set of guidelines for loans to be purchased, and lenders must follow these to the letter if they hope to sell the loan to that particular buyer. Lenders *are* anxious to sell! As one loan officer put it, "The only good loan is a saleable one. An even better loan is one we've already sold!"

Because Fannie Mae has immense buying capability, lenders court her diligently. FNMA guidelines are treated with almost as much reverence as the Ten Commandments. Lenders simply cannot afford to ignore them. And because the FNMA guidelines are based upon economic common sense and prudent banking practices, many other investors (but not all) follow similar rules. That explains the apparent standardization in lending requirements throughout the nation. And that is why it's very difficult to argue with a loan officer... and win.

After you have received your loan, you may or may not be aware of its later sale to an investor. Some lenders continue to service the loan — that is, collect the monthly payments — while in other cases you may be asked to send your payments directly to a new lending institution. In either case, the new investor must certainly live up to the agreement established between you and your original lender.

THE ROLE OF MORTGAGE BROKERS

Throughout this book, I've been including **mortgage brokers** with the institutional lenders, but their role is somewhat different. Instead of *funding* loans — by that I mean providing money for loans — mortgage brokers simply act as agents for other lending institutions. They take loan applications and qualify buyers for the actual lender, an institution which may be located in another city or state. Borrowers who work with mortgage brokers are sometimes surprised to find a different name on their closing documents. They've applied to ABC Services for a loan, and their final loan papers are from XYZ Bank. After closing, XYZ Bank will service the loan, paying a fee to ABC Services, the broker who handled the initial processing. Mortgage brokers have been an asset to the lending market by offering a wide assortment of loans that are not available from local lenders.

SPEEDING UP THE LOAN PROCESS

Obtaining a new loan usually takes from four to eight weeks, and sometimes even longer. The largest portion of that time is spent in verifying the borrower's credit information and in collecting data the lender will need to make a decision. In fact, once this information has been assembled, the loan committee needs very little time to approve the loan, from several hours to a few days at most.

Here's how you can speed up the process, by giving your loan officer a head start on the paperwork. If you arrive at the loan application interview (the *Loan App*) with all the necessary documents and data in hand, you'll shave valuable days off the projected timetable. In this chapter, you'll find a **LOAN APPLICATION CHECKLIST** of items your loan officer will need.

PRE-APPLYING FOR A LOAN

A popular practice these days is for borrowers to *pre-apply* for a loan — that is, to apply for a loan before having an offer accepted. It's even possible to apply before starting your search. This can save some time from the overall loan process, especially where the borrowers have recently lived or worked in another city or state. But because much of the lender's research is pertinent to the home itself, pre-applying usually is not a significant time-saver. It has one advantage, however: borrowers who pre-apply often know exactly the size of loan they are qualified to receive. And if problems with credit reports should crop up, there's plenty of time to deal with them before the rush of closing.

APPLYING FOR AN ASSUMPTION

Blind assumptions usually do not necessitate an interview with the lender. But for other assumptions, lenders often insist that the buyers make formal loan application, as though they were applying for a new loan. In such a case, the same information and documents will be required. While most lenders do not require a new appraisal of the home, some do. If so, a check for the appraisal (and credit report) will be collected at the time of the Loan App.

LOAN APPLICATION CHECKLIST

Here are items your loan officer will require for the Loan Application:

1. **Your checkbook**, for the credit report and appraisal fees

2. **Information about the home:**
   - ☐ a legible, complete copy of the sales agreement
   - ☐ a copy of the earnest money check or note
   - ☐ the last deed and plat map or other documents showing exact legal description of the property
   - ☐ name and phone number of person who can give appraiser access to the home
   - ☐ for FHA and VA loans: copies of heat and utility bills for the past 12 months, or signed statement from seller showing costs

3. **Personal Information** (for applicant and spouse if both incomes are to be counted or if both will take title to the property):
   - ☐ current home address and phone number
   - ☐ previous home address for the past 4 years
   - ☐ birth dates
   - ☐ Social Security Numbers
   - ☐ name and address of current employers
   - ☐ name and address of previous employers (previous 2 years)
   - ☐ for veterans' loans: (VA or FHA/VA) a copy of your discharge paper (DD214)
   - ☐ for VA loans: name and address of your nearest living relative

4. Assets and Liabilities (for applicant and spouse):

- ☐ current gross salary (before deductions)
- ☐ list and amounts of paycheck deductions
- ☐ income for the past 3 years (all sources)
- ☐ if you work on commission: federal income tax returns for the past 3 years
- ☐ if you are (or were) self-employed: federal income tax returns plus profit and loss statements for the past three years (a CPA's signature is often required)
- ☐ record of benefits received, such as Social Security, disability, veteran's benefits
- ☐ names, addresses and account numbers of all banks, S&Ls, credit unions, etc. where you have a savings or checking account, plus the approximate balance of each
- ☐ names, addresses and account numbers of all your credit cards and credit accounts, plus the balance and monthly payments required on each (this includes major credit cards, department store credit cards, plus charge accounts at local businesses)
- ☐ names. addresses, account numbers, monthly payments and balance of any current or previous loans, such as other mortgage loans, car loans, student loans, etc.
- ☐ record of any stocks or bonds that you own plus name and address of brokerage firm that can verify holdings
- ☐ proof of any assets such as cash value life insurance or retirement fund
- ☐ if you receive or pay alimony or child support: a copy of the divorce decree and deposit receipts or other proof
- ☐ an estimate of the value of all your personal property: household goods, clothing, jewelry, hobby equipment, etc.
- ☐ information about any bankruptcy or judgments

"Don't worry, I'll dig up the down payment somewhere," is a statement that guarantees you a quick exit from any loan office. A prospective borrower who doesn't have sufficient cash will be denied a loan. Sounds elementary, but you might be surprised at the number of buyers who stumble here. You see, the funds for your down payment must be sitting in your bank account when you apply for your loan. Or they must be in the form of an asset that can be readily converted to cash — bonds, for instance. But if your accounts do not show a balance large enough to cover the down payment plus closing costs, and no other obvious assets are present, you will have to offer proof of sufficient funds before you receive loan approval.

Perhaps a relative will be giving you the money for the down payment. If so, then the lender will want a **gift letter** from the donor, stating clearly that this is a gift and repayment is not required. Lenders are cautious about approving gift letters. After all, they want to be absolutely certain that a borrower is capable of repaying a loan. There are some definite rules that apply here. first of all, the gift must be from a blood relative. While FHA will allow a gift letter to cover the total down payment, most conventional lenders now require borrowers to have at least a 5% down payment in funds of their own. Additional money for the down payment may then be in the form of a gift. Some lenders make an exception to this rule when the down payment is 20% or larger; then the entire down payment may be a gift.

Lenders want to be absolutely certain that the money you receive from your relative is not a loan in disguise. Loans, with their required payments, affect the amount of your disposable income. So if you do borrow money for part of your down payment, this must be shown on your loan application, with documentation explaining how and when the money is to be repaid. Your loan payments for these funds will be included in the qualifying calculations and may lower your borrowing limit.

SAILING THROUGH LOAN APP

When you have assembled all the necessary documents and information, make an appointment to see the loan officer you have chosen. Because loan applications are complicated, loan officers prefer to complete the form with the prospective borrower sitting close by. During the Loan App, your loan officer will review the terms of the loan you have chosen, and will run calculations to see if you qualify for the size and type of loan you want. You will be given a written estimate of your closing costs and your monthly (or biweekly) payment figures. The loan officer will then fill in the application form using the information you have brought, and will ask you to sign it. At the same time, you will also be asked to sign form letters to your employer, and to the various banks, credit unions, savings and loan associations or mortgage companies where you have an account. These letters will be sent out by your lender to request verification of your employment or banking history.

You must also leave a check for the cost of the credit report and a fee appraisal of the home you're buying. This amount varies with location and the type of appraisal required for your particular loan, but the total expense can often run to $300 or more. Your loan officer can tell you in advance what to expect. The fees for the credit report and appraisal are non-refundable, whether the loan is granted or not. That is why your loan officer takes great care in qualifying you as accurately as possible. Yet even if your loan officer feels that you do qualify for the loan, it may still be denied later by the *loan committee*, the deciding voice in loan approval. Sometimes the results of the credit report, employment and banking verification may darken an otherwise rosy picture.

APPRAISING THE HOME

A fee appraisal of the home is necessary to assure the lender (who must assure the investor) that the property is worth the investment. Just because you've offered to pay $60,000 for the home, and the seller has agreed to this price, doesn't mean that the home is *worth* $60,000. You may have been blinded by love-at-first-sight (it's really worth $50,000), or you may have latched onto the deal of the decade (it's actually worth $70,000). Lenders base their loan amounts on the market value of the home, not on the selling price. You and the seller have decided what you think it's worth; now it's up to the appraiser to give an opinion.

Appraisals *are* simply opinions. Except in areas of look-alike housing, two professional appraisers are likely to give two different estimates of value. However they do follow certain recognized methods for arriving at a figure. The usual method for single-family homes is the **Market Data Approach**. It is somewhat similar to the research you did when you evaluated homes in your Target Area. You compared the home you were considering with other homes in the neighborhood that were on the market or had been sold recently. Appraisers look only at homes similar to yours that have *sold* in recent months. They compare the physical aspects of the homes, as well as the type of financing used for each (different methods of financing often result in different sales prices). If the home you've chosen is near other similar homes, with plenty of recent sales, the appraiser's job is easy. But if you've picked a one-of-a-kind home, or one in a community that's experiencing a slow real estate market, your poor appraiser will have a more difficult time.

If you have done your research thoroughly, you'll have a very good idea of the market value of your home. I hope the appraiser agrees. But if the appraisal comes in low, ask your loan officer for a copy of it. Go over it carefully with your real estate agent to make sure that there are no mistakes. Appraisers are human, after all! One appraisal I checked had fourteen serious errors in it, many of which directly affected the final outcome. If you do find mistakes, call these to the attention of the loan officer, or ask your real estate agent to intervene. Be sure to supply documentation to back up your claim.

ESTIMATING YOUR CLOSING COSTS

As part of your Loan App, your loan officer will give you a written estimate of your closing costs. I emphasize that this is an *estimate* because until you know exactly which day the closing will take place, it is impossible to calculate the closing costs with absolute accuracy. This will, however, be very close to the actual amount you'll be required to pay. In the following chapter, you'll find a **CLOSING COSTS CHART**, indicating costs and fees that may be charged with different types of financing.

TIMETABLE FOR LOAN PROCESSING

Once you've completed the Loan App, you've done your part. From here on, you are at the mercy of the loan officer, the U.S. Postal Service, the credit reporting agency, the appraiser, your bank and your employer's payroll department. How quickly you receive your loan approval will depend upon the speed and efficiency of all of the above. Of course applicants with out-of-state employers or bank accounts can expect a longer wait than those whose verification letters are mailed to local addresses. But in general, the timetable for a typical new loan goes like this:

Day 1	Loan Application
Days 2 – 7	Financial and employment verification letters sent by lender Credit report and appraisal ordered by lender
Days 6 – 14	Appraiser inspects home (written appraisal sent to lender within a week)
Days 15 – 28	Appraisal, credit report and completed verification letters received by lender

When the appraisal, credit report and all the verification letters have been completed and returned, your loan officer will examine your data and put together a *package* for the loan committee. Competent loan officers make sure that a loan package presents the strongest possible case on the applicant's behalf. Sometimes it's necessary to fortify the package with additional information before it goes to loan committee. Often clarification is needed. An example of this might be a credit report showing that you have a car loan, when, in fact, you repaid the loan two months ago. Or perhaps your employment verification failed to indicate the amount of the bonus you receive each year. Your loan officer may ask you, your employer or your creditors for more details.

Once your package is complete, your loan officer will submit it to the loan committee. Usually within one to four days, you will hear one of three answers:

- your loan has been approved, or

- your loan has been conditionally approved, (approved only if you agree to accept certain conditions) or

- your loan has been denied.

Even if your loan has not been approved, most lenders will allow a package to be resubmitted if new supporting information has been received. However your loan application will have a much better chance of survival if the weak spots are fortified before the loan committee finds them.

COUNTDOWN TO CLOSING

After you have received loan approval, your lender's loan processing department prepares the final documents that will be needed to complete the transaction. **STEP NINE** is next: the **closing,** or **settlement,** or **escrow,** as it is called in various parts of the country. Whatever name you give this final wrap-up, the result will be the same — in just a few days, the home will be yours to enjoy!

STEP NINE

UNDERSTAND THE CLOSING

"The universe is merely a fleeting idea in God's mind — a pretty uncomfortable thought, particularly if you've just made a down payment on a house."

Woody Allen

The closing is the last major hurdle between you and your first home. And by the time you've finished reading this chapter, you'll leap right over that hurdle without spraining anything.

When I say **closing**, I'm referring to the grand finale, the time when all the final documents are signed and the home is yours at last. In some parts of the country, this is known as the **settlement** or **escrow**. Just as the name varies, so does the procedure. In some areas, buyers, sellers, their agents, attorneys and the lender's representative gather around the lender's conference table to sign papers, exchange checks, and discuss the inevitable last-minute questions that arise. Elsewhere, closings are private affairs, with the buyers signing papers at one time, the sellers at another, in the escrow office of a title insurance or abstract company, or in some states, real estate firms. For this type of closing, buyers and sellers may never actually meet.

Your real estate agent will see that the details of your closing are arranged. He or she will make sure that the active participants (the lender, the title insurance company, the escrow officer and the attorney) have all received copies of the transaction documents and are carrying out the necessary processing, so that your closing can be scheduled right on time.

However and *wherever* your closing/escrow/settlement is held, the outcome is the same. You will have an opportunity to examine and sign all of the documents pertaining to your financing and the purchase of your home. Be prepared for a mountain of paper, especially if you are financing the home with a new loan. Document after document will require your signature, until you're apt to be overwhelmed by the whole procedure.

But before you find yourself in overwhelming circumstances, take time to prepare for the closing, so that you'll know exactly what to expect. This chapter will give you help in that direction.

EXAMINING THE TITLE

While your loan documents are being prepared, there's still more research to be done. You've made sure that there are no physical defects in the home you'll be buying. Now it's necessary to make certain there are no defects in the chain of title. Problems of this sort can be costly indeed and the title search is a job best left to a professional.

Title is your right to own property. It's an abstract term; a title is not something you can hold in your hand. The actual evidence of your title is the document known as a **deed**. When you buy a home, the seller will sign a deed, conveying the property to you. There are different types of deeds, but the one most commonly used (and most desirable) in real estate transactions is the **warranty deed**, also known as the **general warranty deed**. With this deed, the owner warrants a good, clear title to the property. But your goal, before purchasing, should be to feel absolutely certain that the title *is* good and that you are protected against problems that may appear later.

110

That's exactly why **title insurance** was created. This type of insurance was designed to offer protection against hidden defects in the title. Although title insurance has been with us for over one hundred years, many buyers still play Russian Roulette with their real estate transactions. They cannot believe that anything could cloud their title. So what could go wrong? I'll describe two true situations that happened to close friends of mine.

First, my neighbors discovered, to their horror, that they did not own their front yard and garage — after they'd lived in the home for ten years. Someone else did. The actual owner had recently bought the property at a delinquent tax auction and offered to sell it to my neighbors at close to one hundred times his purchase price! Of course my friends had never received a tax bill, since they were not the owners of record of that parcel. After a long court case, the judge decided in favor of the purchaser. My neighbors had to pay the price, or give up the yard and garage, making their home quite unsaleable. How did this happen? When my neighbors bought their home, they trusted their luck and didn't bother to seek legal advice or have a professional title search made. The lesson they learned from that experience was a very expensive and frustrating one.

The second situation had a happier ending because the owner had a title insurance policy working for him. Several months after he moved into his home, the owner received notice that a lien had been filed against the property. The previous owner had not paid a bill and the creditor was trying (improperly) to collect from the purchaser. Without title insurance, the new owner would have had to engage an attorney, or fend off the lien by himself. But instead, the title insurance company's attorneys took care of the entire matter, at no cost to the owner.

The list of possible title defects is long and frightening, with missing heirs popping out of the woodwork to claim the inheritance, or improperly prepared deeds coming back to haunt the new owner. A title insurance policy makes very good financial sense.

There are some parts of the United States where title insurance is not frequently used, although it is available across the country. If you decide to go without coverage, I strongly recommend that you ask your attorney to do a **title search** for you. The attorney will examine the public records and will issue what is known as a **certificate of title**, a document giving an opinion of the title. While the attorney's examination will disclose recorded liens or claims, it does not include responsibility for *hidden* title defects, such as a forged deed, or an honest recording error. In fact, an attorney's liability is limited to negligence only. That is why title insurance is becoming increasingly popular.

TITLE INSURANCE FOR OWNERS AND LENDERS

There are two different kinds of title insurance — a policy for the **lender** and one for the **owner** (the buyer). These are also known as the **mortgagee's policy** and the **mortgagor's policy**, respectively. Most lenders today want title protection, at least for the value of the loan, and buyers are routinely asked to provide this coverage. Somewhat more expensive is the owner's policy, the policy that protects the buyer. It is customary to ask the seller to pay for this policy, and this is a provision that should be outlined clearly in your offer. Your real estate agent can give you information about title insurance or title examination procedures in your community.

If a title insurance policy is being purchased, you will receive a **preliminary title policy**, or **prelim** as it is nicknamed, well before closing. This policy will indicate the title insurance company's findings, and will list the recorded liens and encumbrances that appear in the public files. Read this policy carefully and notice whether there are any loans or other encumbrances against the property that you were not aware of. Once you purchase the home, you will be liable for these recorded encumbrances; your title insurance policy will exclude these. So if anything listed on your preliminary policy seems questionable or unfamiliar, discuss the policy with your real estate agent or attorney. Do not sign closing documents until you are satisfied that you understand what is included or excluded from your policy.

DO YOU NEED AN ATTORNEY?

Buyers often wonder if they should have an attorney advise and represent them at closing. Again, practice differs throughout the country, but here are a few general guidelines:

- If you're confused about *any* document you're asked to sign, at any stage in the homebuying process, seek legal advice before you sign.

- If you are not protected by title insurance, have an attorney check the title to see that it is clear.

- If the seller is financing your purchase, by means of a contract or private mortgage, it's wise to have your attorney draft the documents.

- If you are using 'sweat equity' to cover all or part of your down payment, ask your attorney to draw up an agreement to cover all aspects of the work.

- If it's customary in your area to have an attorney present at closing (your real estate agent can tell you this), then give the idea careful consideration.

In general, if you have *any* doubts, ask for legal advice.

THE ROLE OF AN ESCROW AGENT

Escrow is the process by which documents and money are held by a neutral party until all the terms and conditions of an agreement have been carried out. **Escrow officers** (also known as **escrow agents**) may be employees of a title insurance company, abstract company or lending institution. In some areas, attorneys or real estate brokers perform escrow duties. The important factor is the escrow agent's neutrality. He or she 'sides' with neither the buyer nor the seller but simply carries out the written instructions that both buyer and seller have agreed to. In the case of your home purchase, the written instructions are in the form of an accepted offer, plus any additional agreements signed by both you and the seller. (Each of these is known as an **addendum**). Your lender, too, issues instructions to the escrow officer regarding the documents for your new loan or assumption.

Escrow agents must follow these written instructions to the letter. They calculate and verify the closing figures, assemble all the necessary closing documents, oversee the closing procedure, record the deed or contract, then disburse the proceeds of the transaction to the seller and real estate firm.

Shortly before closing, the escrow officer will calculate your actual closing costs and will notify you of the amount of the certified check you'll need to bring with you. At the time your offer was written, your real estate agent may have given you a rough estimate of your closing costs. When you applied for your loan, your lender gave you a closer estimate of the fees associated with your financing. But the actual figure, down to the last penny, cannot be calculated until the exact date of closing is known. So many closing costs (such as interest, property taxes and insurance) vary with the closing date. You'll have to accept a close estimate until near closing time.

While closing costs vary with the type of financing you choose and the region where you are buying a home, the chart included in this chapter indicates closing costs you may incur. Ask your lender, real estate agent or escrow officer to explain any of the unfamiliar fees that appear on your estimates.

114

CLOSING COSTS

Here are closing costs which you **may** incur with different types of financing. Ask your loan officer, real estate agent or escrow officer for your specific costs.

	Conventional Loan	FHA Loan	VA Loan	Assumption	Land Sales Contract	Estimated Loan Costs
Appraisal Fee	★	★	★	★		
Credit Report	★	★	★	★		
Loan Fee/Assumption Fee	★	★	★	★		
VA Funding Fee			★			
Discount Points	★	★	★			
Buydown Fee	★	★	★			
Mortgage Insurance Premium	★	★				
Underwriting Fee	★	★	★			
Tax Service Fee	★	★	★			
Survey Fee	★	★	★			
Inspection Fee	★	★	★			
Mortgagee's Title Insurance	★	★	★			
Interest Payment	★	★	★	★		
Down Payment	★	★	★	★	★	
Homeowner's Insurance	★	★	★	★	★	
Tax Pro-rates/Reserves	★	★	★	★	★	
Escrow Fee	★	★	★	★	★	
Attorney's Fee	★	★	★	★	★	
Sales Tax/Transfer Tax	★	★	★	★	★	
Recording Fee	★	★	★	★	★	

A SNEAK PREVIEW OF CLOSING PAPERS

Very few homebuyers read every word of their closing papers before they sign. Who can absorb the small print on a complex document while others are waiting and watching? If you would feel more comfortable having a chance to study the closing papers in advance, ask your lender and escrow agent for sample copies of the documents you'll be expected to sign. You'll be able to ponder over the small print at your leisure.

THE IMPORTANCE OF A WALK-THROUGH

Just before closing, ask your real estate agent to arrange a *walk-through* of your new home. Accompany your agent on a tour of the home for one final inspection. Note whether the home is in substantially the same condition as it was when you made your offer, or if the condition has deteriorated since then. If repairs were to have been made, as part of your agreement, check to see that they have been completed to your satisfaction. It's even a good idea to try built-in appliances to see if they work. With a walk-through, there can be no question later as to whether or not you received the home in the condition you expected. And you'll have better leverage in getting last minute problems solved *before* you sign the final papers.

RECORDING THE DOCUMENTS

For your protection, the deed or contract must be recorded in the county recording office. Other documents will be recorded, too, such as the mortgage or trust deed, and a *satisfaction of mortgage* for any previous loan against the property that was paid off at closing. Your escrow agent will see that these documents are recorded and will send you final recorded copies for your files.

After recording, the home is really and truly yours! Now all that's left is **STEP TEN**. You're ready to move in and enjoy all the benefits of owning your first home.

STEP TEN

ENJOY YOUR FIRST TASTE
OF HOME OWNERSHIP

"There are two things to aim at in life: first, to get what you want; and after that, to enjoy it. Only the wisest of mankind achieve the second."

Logan Pearsall Smith

Possession, they say, is nine-tenths of the law. When you have just bought your first home, *possession* should be *ten*-tenths — a full measure — of enjoyment. After you take possession of your new home, when the furniture is in place and the boxes are unpacked, take time to congratulate yourself on a job well done. You've accomplished a difficult feat: buying one's first home is rarely an easy project.

Now it's time to be sure that you get your full measure of enjoyment out of your purchase. There will be times, when the basement floods or the furnace breaks down, that you'll wish you had a landlord to call. Home ownership brings its share of headaches. But most homeowners wouldn't have it any other way. For them the benefits far outweigh the drawbacks.

The first major benefit is the tax advantage you've instantly acquired. While the Tax Act of 1986 did its best to steamroller the loopholes in the income tax law, it took a detour when it came to the best loophole of all for

117

most Americans. There are still excellent tax benefits to be gained by owning your own home. Interest that you pay on your home mortgage loan or contract is deductible, as are your property taxes. To be certain you're taking the full tax advantages of home ownership, ask your accountant for advice.

Secondly, there's a benefit you don't have to fill out forms to obtain: equity. With inflation and rising housing prices, your home will be *working* for you. Sit back and watch your investment grow in value. Or make wise improvements (with your real estate agent's advice) to increase your equity at a faster pace.

Finally there's that splendid feeling of independence. It's that great American love of freedom and you've just helped yourself to your share! This is *your* home and you're perfectly free to do what you like with it — within legal bounds, of course. That's just one more advantage of home ownership.

My goal in this book has been to show you how to reach *your* goal, by the easiest, straightest and safest path. With guidance and plenty of perseverence, you've worked your way through the ten steps in the homebuying process until you successfully accomplished what you set out to do: you bought a home! I hope it will give you, in addition to the other benefits I mentioned, many years of happiness. Congratulations — you've done it!

APPENDIX I
LOAN AMORTIZATION CHART

Use this chart to determine what your monthly principal and interest payment will be. Real estate loan payments are amortized over the term of the loan. That is, the payments are calculated to include the correct amount of principal and interest so that the loan balance will be zero at the end of the term.

Step 1: Find the applicable interest rate in the top row.

Step 2: Find the term of the loan in the column on the left.

Step 3: Trace down the rate column and across the term row to the square where the two meet. Remember this factor.

Step 4: Move the decimal point in your loan amount three places to the left. Example: $57,850. becomes 57.850.

Step 5: Multiply this number by the factor you have found on the chart.

Example: A 12% loan with a term of 30 years would have a factor of 10.29 according to the chart. If the loan balance is $57,850, we would multiply 57.850 by 10.29 and find that our monthly payment (principal and interest) would be $595.28.

YEAR	6.00	6.25	6.50	6.75	7.00	7.25	7.50	7.75	8.00	8.25	8.50 %
1	86.07	86.18	86.30	86.41	86.53	86.64	86.76	86.87	86.99	87.10	87.22
	44.32	44.43	44.55	44.66	44.77	44.89	45.00	45.11	45.23	45.34	45.46
	30.42	30.54	30.65	30.76	30.88	30.99	31.11	31.22	31.34	31.45	31.57
	23.49	23.60	23.71	23.83	23.95	24.06	24.18	24.30	24.41	24.53	24.65
5	19.33	19.45	19.57	19.68	19.80	19.92	20.04	20.16	20.28	20.40	20.52
	16.57	16.69	16.81	16.93	17.05	17.17	17.29	17.41	17.53	17.66	17.78
	14.61	14.73	14.85	14.97	15.09	15.22	15.34	15.46	15.59	15.71	15.84
	13.14	13.26	13.39	13.51	13.63	13.76	13.88	14.01	14.14	14.26	14.39
	12.01	12.13	12.25	12.38	12.51	12.63	12.76	12.89	13.02	13.15	13.28
10	11.10	11.23	11.35	11.48	11.61	11.74	11.87	12.00	12.13	12.27	12.40
	10.37	10.49	10.62	10.75	10.88	11.02	11.15	11.28	11.42	11.55	11.69
	9.76	9.89	10.02	10.15	10.28	10.42	10.55	10.69	10.82	10.96	11.10
	9.25	9.38	9.51	9.65	9.78	9.92	10.05	10.19	10.33	10.47	10.61
	8.81	8.95	9.08	9.22	9.35	9.49	9.63	9.77	9.91	10.06	10.20
15	8.44	8.57	8.71	8.85	8.99	9.13	9.27	9.41	9.56	9.70	9.85
	8.11	8.25	8.39	8.53	8.67	8.81	8.96	9.10	9.25	9.40	9.54
	7.83	7.97	8.11	8.25	8.40	8.54	8.69	8.83	8.98	9.13	9.28
	7.58	7.72	7.87	8.01	8.16	8.30	8.45	8.60	8.75	8.90	9.05
	7.36	7.50	7.65	7.79	7.94	8.09	8.24	8.39	8.55	8.70	8.85
20	7.16	7.31	7.46	7.60	7.75	7.90	8.06	8.21	8.36	8.52	8.68
	6.99	7.14	7.28	7.43	7.58	7.74	7.89	8.05	8.20	8.36	8.52
	6.83	6.98	7.13	7.28	7.43	7.59	7.75	7.90	8.06	8.22	8.38
	6.69	6.84	6.99	7.14	7.30	7.46	7.61	7.77	7.93	8.10	8.26
	6.56	6.71	6.87	7.02	7.18	7.34	7.50	7.66	7.82	7.98	8.15
25	6.44	6.60	6.75	6.91	7.07	7.23	7.39	7.55	7.72	7.88	8.05
	6.34	6.49	6.65	6.81	6.97	7.13	7.29	7.46	7.63	7.79	7.96
	6.24	6.40	6.56	6.72	6.88	7.04	7.21	7.37	7.54	7.71	7.88
	6.15	6.31	6.47	6.63	6.80	6.96	7.13	7.30	7.47	7.64	7.81
	6.07	6.23	6.39	6.56	6.72	6.89	7.06	7.23	7.40	7.57	7.75
30	6.00	6.16	6.32	6.49	6.65	6.82	6.99	7.16	7.34	7.51	7.69

YEAR

	8.75	9.00	9.25	9.50	9.75	10.00	10.25	10.50	10.75	11.00	11.25 %
1	87.34	87.45	87.57	87.68	87.80	87.92	88.03	88.15	88.27	88.38	88.50
	45.57	45.68	45.80	45.91	46.03	46.14	46.26	46.38	46.49	46.61	46.72
	31.68	31.80	31.92	32.03	32.15	32.27	32.38	32.50	32.62	32.74	32.86
	24.77	24.89	25.00	25.12	25.24	25.36	25.48	25.60	25.72	25.85	25.97
5	20.64	20.76	20.88	21.00	21.12	21.25	21.37	21.49	21.62	21.74	21.87
	17.90	18.03	18.15	18.27	18.40	18.53	18.65	18.78	18.91	19.03	19.16
	15.96	16.09	16.22	16.34	16.47	16.60	16.73	16.86	16.99	17.12	17.25
	14.52	14.65	14.78	14.91	15.04	15.17	15.31	15.44	15.57	15.71	15.84
	13.41	13.54	13.68	13.81	13.94	14.08	14.21	14.35	14.49	14.63	14.76
10	12.53	12.67	12.80	12.94	13.08	13.22	13.35	13.49	13.63	13.78	13.92
	11.82	11.96	12.10	12.24	12.38	12.52	12.66	12.80	12.95	13.09	13.24
	11.24	11.38	11.52	11.66	11.81	11.95	12.10	12.24	12.39	12.54	12.68
	10.75	10.90	11.04	11.19	11.33	11.48	11.63	11.78	11.92	12.08	12.23
	10.34	10.49	10.64	10.78	10.93	11.08	11.23	11.38	11.54	11.69	11.85
15	9.99	10.14	10.29	10.44	10.59	10.75	10.90	11.05	11.21	11.37	11.52
	9.69	9.85	10.00	10.15	10.30	10.46	10.62	10.77	10.93	11.09	11.25
	9.43	9.59	9.74	9.90	10.05	10.21	10.37	10.53	10.69	10.85	11.02
	9.21	9.36	9.52	9.68	9.84	10.00	10.16	10.32	10.49	10.65	10.82
	9.01	9.17	9.33	9.49	9.65	9.81	9.98	10.14	10.31	10.47	10.64
20	8.84	9.00	9.16	9.32	9.49	9.65	9.82	9.98	10.15	10.32	10.49
	8.68	8.85	9.01	9.17	9.34	9.51	9.68	9.85	10.02	10.19	10.36
	8.55	8.71	8.88	9.04	9.21	9.38	9.55	9.73	9.90	10.07	10.25
	8.43	8.59	8.76	8.93	9.10	9.27	9.44	9.62	9.79	9.97	10.15
	8.32	8.49	8.66	8.83	9.00	9.17	9.35	9.52	9.70	9.88	10.06
25	8.22	8.39	8.56	8.74	8.91	9.09	9.26	9.44	9.62	9.80	9.98
	8.13	8.31	8.48	8.66	8.83	9.01	9.19	9.37	9.55	9.73	9.91
	8.06	8.23	8.41	8.58	8.76	8.94	9.12	9.30	9.49	9.67	9.85
	7.99	8.16	8.34	8.52	8.70	8.88	9.06	9.25	9.43	9.61	9.80
	7.92	8.10	8.28	8.46	8.64	8.82	9.01	9.19	9.38	9.57	9.75
30	7.87	8.05	8.23	8.41	8.59	8.78	8.96	9.15	9.33	9.52	9.71

YEAR

	11.50	11.75	12.00	12.25	12.50	12.75	13.00	13.25	13.50	13.75	14.00 %
1	88.62	88.73	88.85	88.97	89.08	89.20	89.32	89.43	89.55	89.67	89.79
	46.84	46.96	47.07	47.19	47.31	47.42	47.54	47.66	47.78	47.89	48.01
	32.98	33.10	33.21	33.33	33.45	33.57	33.69	33.81	33.94	34.06	34.18
	26.09	26.21	26.33	26.46	26.58	26.70	26.83	26.95	27.08	27.20	27.33
5	21.99	22.12	22.24	22.37	22.50	22.63	22.75	22.88	23.01	23.14	23.27
	19.29	19.42	19.55	19.68	19.81	19.94	20.07	20.21	20.34	20.47	20.61
	17.39	17.52	17.65	17.79	17.92	18.06	18.19	18.33	18.46	18.60	18.74
	15.98	16.12	16.25	16.39	16.53	16.67	16.81	16.95	17.09	17.23	17.37
	14.90	15.04	15.18	15.33	15.47	15.61	15.75	15.90	16.04	16.19	16.33
10	14.06	14.20	14.35	14.49	14.64	14.78	14.93	15.08	15.23	15.38	15.53
	13.38	13.53	13.68	13.83	13.98	14.13	14.28	14.43	14.58	14.73	14.89
	12.83	12.98	13.13	13.29	13.44	13.59	13.75	13.90	14.06	14.21	14.37
	12.38	12.53	12.69	12.84	13.00	13.15	13.31	13.47	13.63	13.79	13.95
	12.00	12.16	12.31	12.47	12.63	12.79	12.95	13.11	13.28	13.44	13.60
15	11.68	11.84	12.00	12.16	12.33	12.49	12.65	12.82	12.98	13.15	13.32
	11.41	11.57	11.74	11.90	12.07	12.23	12.40	12.57	12.74	12.91	13.08
	11.18	11.35	11.51	11.68	11.85	12.02	12.19	12.36	12.53	12.70	12.87
	10.98	11.15	11.32	11.49	11.66	11.83	12.00	12.18	12.35	12.53	12.70
	10.81	10.98	11.15	11.33	11.50	11.67	11.85	12.03	12.20	12.38	12.56
20	10.66	10.84	11.01	11.19	11.36	11.54	11.72	11.89	12.07	12.25	12.44
	10.54	10.71	10.89	11.06	11.24	11.42	11.60	11.78	11.96	12.15	12.33
	10.42	10.60	10.78	10.96	11.14	11.32	11.50	11.69	11.87	12.05	12.24
	10.33	10.51	10.69	10.87	11.05	11.23	11.42	11.60	11.79	11.97	12.16
	10.24	10.42	10.60	10.79	10.97	11.16	11.34	11.53	11.72	11.91	12.10
25	10.16	10.35	10.53	10.72	10.90	11.09	11.28	11.47	11.66	11.85	12.04
	10.10	10.28	10.47	10.66	10.84	11.03	11.22	11.41	11.60	11.80	11.99
	10.04	10.23	10.41	10.60	10.79	10.98	11.17	11.37	11.56	11.75	11.95
	9.99	10.18	10.37	10.56	10.75	10.94	11.13	11.32	11.52	11.71	11.91
	9.94	10.13	10.32	10.52	10.71	10.90	11.09	11.29	11.48	11.68	11.88
30	9.90	10.09	10.29	10.48	10.67	10.87	11.06	11.26	11.45	11.65	11.85

YEAR

APPENDIX II

QUALIFYING FOR A LOAN

The following worksheet will help you calculate the approximate size of loan you'll be qualified to receive. While there is remarkable similarity in lending standards throughout the nation, rules do vary somewhat from loan to loan. This worksheet is a very good starting point, however. It will give you an estimate of where you stand in financial matters, and will help you decide the price range of homes you'll be able to afford.

Before the calculations begin, you'll need to assemble some information. A quick call to a lending institution or your real estate agent should provide all the necessary figures. Here's what you'll need:

• What's the interest rate on new loans?
Find out what the current rate is on the type of loan you're interested in. Not sure yet which type? Try calculating your borrowing power for both a fixed-rate 30-year loan and an ARM, to note the differences.

• Will mortgage insurance be required?
If so, what will the monthly premium be? The Private Mortgage Insurance chart in STEP FIVE will give you an approximate amount for this estimate.

• What would the property taxes cost?
You'll need to have a rough idea of the *monthly* cost of property taxes for your new home. Your real estate agent can give you some sample tax figures for different homes in different neighborhoods. Pick one you think may be close to the type of home you'll buy. This is simply an estimate and an error in the tax figure won't greatly affect the outcome.

• What is the cost of homeowner's insurance?
Again, you'll just need a ballpark figure: how much is insurance likely to cost *per month* for your new home? Real estate agents often can quote approximate figures, based on past experience, or ask your insurance agent.

Qualifying is a two-step process. Before you use the following worksheet, reread the **Rule of Thumb for Loan Qualification** on page 24. Note that the income figures used are for gross monthly income, that is, income *before* taxes or other deductions have been subtracted. Remember, too, that only regular predictable income may be counted. That rules out many year-end bonuses, unless they are predictable and guaranteed by the employer. Commissions or non-salary income may be used if you can show that you've consistently earned a certain amount and that it's likely to continue.

Use a calculator to help you estimate *both* of your qualifying ratios. Expect different results from each one; often the first ratio produces a much higher loan amount than the second. But which one will the lender use? Here are the guidelines:

• *If the maximum loan amount on the First Ratio exceeds that on the Second Ratio, the latter (smaller) amount will usually be your top borrowing limit.*

• *If the maximum loan amount on the Second Ratio exceeds that of the First Ratio, pat yourself on the back. Your total debts are low. In this case, the lender may possibly increase your First Ratio percentage, to 30% or even 32%, and the new First Ratio figure will be used as your maximum loan amount.*

LOAN QUALIFICATION WORKSHEET

Housing Cost Ratio — 'First Ratio':

Gross Monthly Income . . . . $ . . . .
Multiply by . . . .   x .28 *
_____

A.   Maximum allowed for housing costs . . . $ . . . .

Monthly cost of:
   Property Taxes . . . . $ . . . .
   Homeowner's Insurance . . . . . $ . . . .
   Mortgage Insurance . . . . $ . . . .
   Association Fees . . . . $ . . . .
_____

B.   Total . . . . $ . . . .

Subtract Line B from Line A: Line A: $ . . . .
                            minus Line B: $ . . . .
_____

C.   Maximum allowed for monthly
    principal and interest . . . . $ . . . .

Loan Data:
   Interest Rate . . . . %
   Term of loan . . . . years
D.   Amortization Factor . . . .
    (use chart in Appendix)

Divide Line C by Line D:
E. $ . . . . ÷ . . . . = $ . . . .

Line E is the maximum loan amount determined by the
Housing Cost Ratio.

★ For 95% LTV conventional loans, use .25

Total Debt Service Ratio — 'Second Ratio':

Multiply your gross monthly income by .36: *

   Gross monthly income . . . . $ . . . .

                                          x .36 *

                                        _____

F.   Maximum allowed for housing costs
       plus total debts . . . . $ . . . .

Total monthly debts:

   Property taxes . . . . $ . . . .
   Homeowner's Insurance . . . . . $ . . . .
   Mortgage Insurance . . . . $ . . . .
   Association Fees . . . . $ . . . .
   Car Payment . . . . $ . . . .
   Other Loan Payments . . . . $ . . . .
   Total Credit Card Payment . . . $ . . . .
   Alimony/Child Support . . . . $ . . . .
   Other monthly payments . . . . . $ . . . .

                               _____

G.   Total monthly debts . . . . $ . . . .

Subtract Line G from Line F: Line F: $ . . . .
                                minus Line G: $ . . . .

                                      _____

H.   Maximum principal and
       and interest payments . . . . $ . . . .

Divide Line H by the Amortization Factor (Line D)

I. $ . . . . ÷ . . . . = $ . . . .

Line I is the maximum loan amount as determined by the Total Debt Service Ratio. Study the instructions preceeding this worksheet to interpret the results of your calculations.

★ For 95% LTV conventional loans, use .33

INDEX